The Five Faces of Genius

The Five Faces of Genius

THE SKILLS TO MASTER

IDEAS AT WORK

Annette Moser-Wellman

VIKING

VIKING
Published by the Penguin Group
Penguin Putnam Inc., 375 Hudson Street,
New York, New York 10014, U.S.A.
Penguin Books Ltd, 27 Wrights Lane,
London W8 5TZ, England
Penguin Books Australia Ltd, Ringwood,
Victoria, Australia
Penguin Books Canada Ltd, 10 Alcorn Avenue,
Toronto, Ontario, Canada M4V 3B2
Penguin Books (N.Z.) Ltd, 182–190 Wairau Road,
Auckland 10, New Zealand

Penguin Books Ltd, Registered Offices:
Harmondsworth, Middlesex, England

First published in 2001 by Viking Penguin,
a member of Penguin Putnam Inc.

1   3   5   7   9   10   8   6   4   2

Library of Congress Cataloging-in-Publication Data
Moser-Wellman, Annette.
The five faces of genius : the skills to master ideas at work / Annette Moser-Wellman.
p.   cm.
Includes index.
ISBN 0-670-89477-X
1. Creative ability in business.   I. Title: Master ideas at work.   II. Title.
HD53 .M67   2001
650.1—dc21   00-068585

This book is printed on acid-free paper. ∞

Printed in the United States of America
Set in Bembo
Designed by Jaye Zimet

For James
Whose words are under the rocks from the basement of time

ACKNOWLEDGMENTS

There seems no way to separate the writing of a book from the living of a life, so in thanking those who contributed to this effort, I find myself remembering the spirits of those who have influenced me.

To the many colleagues and clients who have taught me the satisfaction of an idea wrested from the heavens, may you each find your signature here.

Thank you to Jane von Mehren and Jennifer Ehmann at Viking for their tireless energy in the shaping of the manuscript. And to my agent, Jan Miller, for her insight, vigilance, and belief in this project.

For their enduring grace, perseverance, and generosity, I thank those who contributed mightily to the ideas here: Marianne Ahern, Terri Alexander, Peter Barnard, Howard Behar, Colette Boeker, Carolyn Harper, Jane Melvin, Carla Paonessa, Barbara Price-Martin, Jim Reynolds, Stacey Riley, Tina Sellers, James K. Wellman Sr., and George Wishart.

And to my mentors in life and work who believed in me and my dreams, Bruce Larson, Steve Hayner, Bob Lipsky, Jerry Reitman, and Tom Collinger.

To my family for their abiding love. To my sister, Deborah Moser-Donlen, for her steadfast care and support. To the memory of my father, Alan Malloy Moser, who taught me the joy of the hunt. To my two daughters, Constance Moser Wellman and Georgia Moser Wellman, in whose creative spirits I rejoice daily.

To my mother, Elizabeth Eileen Moser, whose buoyant spirit and life, intuition and genius will continue to bless others for generations to come.

And finally to my husband, James K. Wellman Jr. He has been my rock and his obsession with truth guides me still.

CONTENTS

The Five Faces of Genius

I

Finding the Business
Genius Within

"It is my business to create."

—WILLIAM BLAKE

HOW did Albert Einstein get the idea for the theory of relativity? What was Georgia O'Keeffe's inspiration for her paintings? How did Andy Grove create the computer giant Intel? Have you ever wondered how history's best got their ideas?

Most of us believe geniuses are in a league of their own. What we don't realize is that these highly creative people use skills we all can learn. People aren't genius; ideas are—and each of us is capable of our own breakthrough ideas.

Here are the thinking skills of some of the most highly inventive people in history—Wolfgang Amadeus Mozart, Frank Lloyd Wright, Leonardo da Vinci, and more. When you understand their path to ideas— how they developed breakthroughs—you'll be able to master your imagination in business. You will discover your creative style—how *your* imagination operates and how to become an idea leader. You'll learn to be a more vital member of your team and to ensure that your ideas see the light of day within your organization. You will discover the parts of *you* that are genius.

Your company needs your genius. We are in a business renaissance, and as in a renaissance, artists, scientists, poets, and thinkers are at the forefront of change. They master possibility, paint on empty canvases, and define the rules of the next age. To lead the changes in business today, you need to think like an artist and master your imagination. Your currency is your ideas.

Here's how I learned the importance of ideas. In the mid-1990s I was a successful manager at a world-renowned advertising agency. Yet, I was looking toward the future and wanted to know how I could accelerate my performance and advance within the company. A trusted colleague was on his way to a new job and I asked him for some honest feedback. What I heard shocked me.

"Jack, tell me. What can I do to improve my work with the team?"

"Well, Annette. You're smart. You're a great manager. You get things done. But you are too focused on 'strategy.' You spend too much time thinking about the problem. The team wants your creative solutions. What are your *ideas*? You need to increase your facility with ideas."

Increase my facility with ideas? I couldn't believe it! I thought my imagination was pretty good—I'd been using it for years. But his words haunted me: not "strategy," but "ideas." I had to admit, Jack was right. I often tried to understand, even argue, about *what* needed to be done instead of how to *create ideas* to get there. How could I increase the quality and quantity of my ideas at work? To be more successful at work, I would have to learn to think more creatively.

I decided to learn about creativity from the best. If I could understand the mental architecture—the thinking skills—of the most highly creative people in history, perhaps I could become more inventive at work. I could sit at the feet of genius and learn to improve my business imagination. I began poring over the innovations of the most well-respected artists, scientists, inventors, and business geniuses of history. With each one I asked, "How did this mind make the contribution? What were the mental principles at work that led to the breakthrough?"

What I found inspired and changed me. I discovered that the creative mind is the same no matter where you find it—in art, in dance, in science—even in business. It took the same skills for Robert Frost to write a poem or for Bob Dylan to write a ballad as it did for Howard Schultz to create the idea for the Starbucks empire or for Ray Kroc to reinvent American dining when he franchised McDonald's. *The same tools of invention used by artists and scientists to create their breakthroughs are used by business people to create breakthroughs in industry.* I had found where art meets business.

I laid the examples of breakthroughs over my desk. As I studied, five common principles of creativity emerged. I even gave them names so I could remember them: the Seer, the Observer, the Alchemist, the Fool, and the Sage. I called the framework the Five Faces of Genius: the mental architecture—the thinking skills—behind some of the greatest contributions in history.

I put the power of the Five Faces of Genius to work at the agency, and the framework became my toolbox for creative thinking. Every time I began working on a project or had to solve a problem, I'd run through the principles in my mind. Immediately I felt the results. I started mastering ideas—sales ideas, marketing ideas, ideas for my clients' businesses, ideas for my firm's business. I stopped worrying about smart answers and started looking for creative answers. I began hearing the compliment, "You never come to me without an idea." I relied not just on my head but also on my intuition and ingenuity to solve problems. *I stopped living like a business manager and began living like an artist.* I began to find a part of the creative genius within me.

As I shared the framework with friends, co-workers, and colleagues, they immediately saw how the Five Faces of Genius would help them. I heard, "I need to find a way to be more creative in what I do at work. Can you teach me?" I heard, "My customer is not just paying for my service, they expect ideas, too." Some told me "idea development" was now a part of their performance evaluation. "I need to figure out how to be more imaginative in my job." My struggle wasn't just my own. It was the same struggle for a generation of other managers. The information economy had changed the landscape of business, and more of us realized the importance of being an idea champion at work.

Today, I am the founder and president of a company called FireMark, which teaches business people to think more creatively using the Five Faces of Genius. Our clients include such renowned and diverse companies as Coca-Cola, Andersen Consulting, Kraft Foods, and Starbucks. My company helps others use the skills to discover new ideas—the uncharted territory of the business—and teaches them how to bring their imagination to work.

In these pages you'll find skills to master breakthrough in the idea economy—how to navigate your imagination and find a deeper energy for your work. A seminar participant says it best, "When I began to master all the Five Faces of Genius skills, I found I had creative powers I never knew I had. Now when I get my group together at work, say to come up with ways to grow our business, I ask the questions the Faces would ask and it helps us dream big. I am enjoying being the 'idea ambassador.' My job is much more fun and meaningful to me."

Now, some of you are saying, "But my management doesn't want imaginative solutions. I'm just expected to follow directions." Or, "My job description is about getting things done." Or, "My team has good ideas; getting them through the organization is the hardest part." And this may be true. There is no denying that the organization corrals innovation, but this is what I want you to know: *The most valuable resource you bring to your work and to your firm is your creativity.* More than what you get done, more than the role you play, more than your title, more than your "output"—it's your ideas that matter. In a business renaissance, when a leading firm can crumble in a minute (Boston Chicken) and another be born in an instant (Amazon.com), even your firm needs business artists.

To become a business artist you don't have to put toys in your office or shoot your colleagues with Nerf guns. You don't have to have the word "creative" in your title. You simply have to commit to finding your genius within. You have a creative spirit worth nurturing. *Dedicate yourself to discovering it.*

Get ready for some of the most valuable skills you may ever learn. The Five Faces of Genius are the raw rubrics of creativity, and once you know them you can apply them to your business challenges. Principles that can help you master your life at work and even your life. We live in an age of change. Don't be a person who responds to change. Be the person who creates it.

The poet William Blake claimed it was his business to create. It is your business to create as well. It is finally what you create, what you contribute, what you call into being at work, that will be your personal legacy. And legacies are not just for artists, philosophers, or Nobel Prize winners alone. A creative legacy is your birthright, too.

You and I spend more time working than any other single activity in our lives. Work is exactly the place that demands the most from us but often where we expect the least. But when you pioneer creativity in your work, you find your creative spirit, and you can transform your soul and change the lives of those around you. The world is waiting to discover your genius. Begin here.

II

The Five Faces of Genius

> *"Genius is at first the ability*
> *to receive discipline."*
> —GEORGE ELIOT

There's a disease rampant in most corporations. I call it the Hurry Scurry Syndrome. When confronted with challenges at work, we either Hurry—try to fix it fast, put together a brainstorming session; or Scurry—delegate the problem to a colleague, subordinate, consultant, or a committee. While trying to do the right thing, we overlook the deepest resource of all—our imagination.

Few of us have been trained in imagination. Most of us stumble around in the dark when it comes to figuring out how to navigate ideas and come up with creative solutions. As one manager confessed to me, "I don't have a clue how my imagination works."

When trying to understand my business imagination, I researched and interviewed forty-five artists and scientists and fifty-two business people. I found highly creative people are dedicated to ideas. They don't rely on their talent alone; they rely on their discipline. Their imagination is like a second skin. They know how to manipulate it to its fullest.

Here are the Five Faces of Genius—the five mental skills mastered by history's greatest. As I said, the mental architecture of breakthrough. To begin to understand your imagination, see how you can recognize yourself in the following thinking styles.

THE SEER: THE POWER TO IMAGE

 Seers see pictures in their mind's eye, and these pictures become the impetus for ingenious ideas. In the same way that someone can imagine his team's final jump shot at the buzzer or how his living room would look with a new color of paint, highly creative people use the skill of the seer to imagine new ideas. Seers are guided by the images in their mind's eye, visualize in great detail, and are able to manipulate these images along the way to maximize their impact and expand their ideas. Mozart describes his Seer moment: "When I am, as it were, completely myself, entirely alone, and of good cheer . . . Provided I am not disturbed, my subject enlarges itself, becomes methodized and defined, and the whole, though it be long, stands almost complete and finished in my mind so that I can survey it, like a fine picture or a beautiful statue, at a glance." The image leads to the breakthrough.

THE OBSERVER: THE POWER TO NOTICE DETAIL

 Observers notice the details of the world around them and collect them to construct a new idea. They scan their environment for interesting information and use this data to create breakthroughs. Observers stand in awe of the world around them, and its beauty is a source of inspiration. They cherish the details and are driven by their unrelenting curiosity. When Walt Disney took his young daughter to play in the park, he noticed the details around him: the adults looked bored, the rides were run-down, and the ride operators were unfriendly. He thought, "Wouldn't it be fun if there was a place where kids and adults could play together?" And from those initial observations he hatched the idea for his theme parks.

THE ALCHEMIST: THE POWER TO CONNECT DOMAINS

Alchemists bring together separate domains—different ideas, disciplines, or systems of thought—and connect them in a unique way to develop breakthrough ideas. The Alchemists' insights come from borrowing or even stealing ideas. They are motivated to invent by a broad range of interests, and they lead lives that connect work and play. The architect Frank Lloyd Wright created the most original buildings in the history of American architecture by using the techniques of the Alchemist. His genius was in marrying the design of the building with the nature of the site. With their seamless integration, he created a breakthrough.

THE FOOL: THE POWER TO CELEBRATE WEAKNESS

The most complex Face, the Fool celebrates weakness. Fools practice three related skills: excelling at inversion, seeing the sense in absurdity, and having unending perseverance. The Fool scientist Roy Plunkett was trying to come up with a new configuration of a chlorofluorocarbon. He accidentally set a can of the chemical on the laboratory radiator. When he found it in the morning, the chlorofluorocarbon had polymerized and created a hard resistant surface on the bottom of the can. Instead of throwing it away and calling it a failure, he analyzed the accident. This mishap was the birth of a new product called Teflon. For the Fool, invention happens through redeeming weakness.

THE SAGE: THE POWER TO SIMPLIFY

Sages use the power of simplification as the primary means to inspiration. They reduce problems to their essence and in the process create an ingenious idea. Simplicity is their credo. Also, Sages look to history as a source of creative insight. They honor the past and find insights in what has happened before. One of the fathers of American photography, Alfred Stieglitz, was a master

Sage. Enchanted with Dutch painter Jan Vermeer, who painted some three hundred years earlier, Stieglitz drew inspiration from Vermeer's style and created entirely new photographs based on the lessons he gleaned from Vermeer compositions.

Identify Your Creative Style: Your Face of Genius

Think now for a moment about how you get ideas. Do you visualize solutions? Or try to simplify the problem to its essence? What works for you?

Each of us develops ideas using different creative styles. When you start to maneuver your imagination, to pursue an idea, you begin in a uniquely personal way. Some of us pay attention to the first vision that pops into our head. Others think of similar situations we've confronted and use that as a starting block.

The truth is most of us are a little like Pavlov's dogs when it comes to our creative styles. Because we've had some good results in the past, we push our "nose" of imagination against the same spot to get a treat again and again. That's how the habit starts.

I call this the "one creative skill" habit, and it is easy to recognize when we think about our colleagues and how they approach problems. Do you have a co-worker who makes you laugh with his wild, outrageous ideas? He may be relying on his Fool skills. Does your boss remember how she solved similar problems at a former company? The Alchemist may be at work here. Most people consistently start at the same place when coming up with their ideas. We get comfortable with our own style and venturing away from it feels strange and awkward. Do you have a one-skill habit?

You can break the habit. When you become aware of how you navigate your imagination, you can identify your primary creative skills and selectively add new ones. This is the heart of the Five Faces of Genius model. Through the book I'll be helping you identify your profile— which of the Five Faces of Genius skills you use most. *Then I will show you how to master all five.* Highly creative individuals use all Five Faces of Genius. By learning to supplement your dominant creative style with the other Faces of Genius, you will develop a crucial portfolio of creative thinking skills.

The following quiz will help you discover how you are currently using your imagination. Once you've completed the quiz, I'll show you your skills within the Five Faces of Genius framework.

THE FIVE FACES OF GENIUS PROFILER

Please answer the questions below. The most accurate results come when you move quickly through the questions and answer with your first response. Try not to spend too much time on any one question.

1. When navigating in the car, I prefer to
   a. follow a map
   b. follow written directions

2. At parties, I am more likely to
   a. be a part of the action
   b. watch the action

3. I learn more by
   a. talking with others
   b. studying by myself ME

4. I would prefer to win an award for
   a. Most Likely to Succeed
   b. Best Sense of Humor

5. I would rather have
   a. a few fine clothes
   b. many nice clothes JAH

6. When recalling a conversation, it is easier for me to
   a. visualize the scene JAH
   b. remember parts of a dialogue ME

7. "I often find myself wondering why things are the way they are."
    a. This statement does not describe me.
    b. This statement describes me.

8. People seem to me to be
    a. more similar than different
    b. more different than similar

9. "I drive my friends crazy with my sense of humor."
    a. This statement does not describe me. *ME*
    b. This statement describes me.

10. I am more likely to be interested in
    a. history
    b. psychology *ME*

11. When I recall my childhood, I
    a. see pictures in my mind's eye
    b. remember stories

12. When I find a small scratch on my car or furniture, I am more likely to
    a. forget it quickly
    b. wonder how it happened

13. I would prefer to know
    a. something about many areas
    b. a lot about one area

14. "I find myself wondering what the opposite idea might be."
    a. This statement does not describe me.
    b. This statement describes me.

15. I prefer to
    a. edit
    b. write

16. When describing the scene of an accident, I would tend to
  a. narrate the picture in my mind
  b. chronicle events

17. I am more likely to be
  a. irritated by detail
  b. intrigued by detail

18. I feel the subjects I studied in school were
  a. valuable to my professional career
  b. not very valuable to my professional career

19. "My ideas are a little wacky compared to others."
  a. This statement does not describe me.
  b. This statement describes me.

20. When conversing with others, I tend to appreciate
  a. brevity of thought
  b. nuance of thought

21. "Once I see something in my head, it's almost impossible for me to forget it."
  a. This statement describes me.
  b. This statement does not describe me.

22. I would be more interested in
  a. working for a political campaign
  b. writing political commentary

23. I feel it is more important to
  a. pay attention to what is around me
  b. pay attention to what is within me

24. "When I believe in an idea, I will push it no matter what the cost."
  a. This statement does not describe me.
  b. This statement describes me.

25. I prefer
    a. simple truth
    b. complex meaning

26. "I often find myself 'framing' shots I'd like to photograph."
    a. This statement describes me.
    b. This statement does not describe me.

27. "My curiosity feels insatiable."
    a. This statement does not describe me.
    b. This statement describes me.

28. When others speak, I often say in response, "That reminds me of . . ."
    a. This statement describes me.
    b. This statement does not describe me.

29. I like the phrase "Question authority."
    a. I disagree with this statement.
    b. I agree with this statement.

30. "I like the minimalist approach."
    a. This statement describes me.
    b. This statement does not describe me.

31. "I like to shut my eyes and see the picture in my mind."
    a. This statement describes me.
    b. This statement does not describe me.

32. "I find the 'fine print' intriguing."
    a. This statement does not describe me.
    b. This statement describes me.

33. I am more likely to say
    a. "That person is sharp as a tack."
    b. "That person is very bright."

34. If I were on the show *Seinfeld*, I would likely be cast as
   a. Jerry Seinfeld
   b. Kramer ⌐

35. When describing an event to another, I usually err on the side of providing
   a. not enough information √A H
   b. too much information ⌐

36. "My memory is almost photographic."
   (a.) This statement describes me.
   b. This statement does not describe me.

37. When watching something I enjoyed for a second time, I am more likely to
   a. become bored
   (b.) learn something ⌐

38. I prefer to read
   a. a lot of magazines about different areas
   (b.) a few magazines in depth

39. "If someone asked me at the end of the day what funny things happened today, I could talk all night."
   a. This statement does not describe me.
   (b.) This statement describes me.

40. "I would enjoy living for a time in an Amish community."
   a. This statement describes me.
   (b.) This statement does not describe me.

Quiz Key
- Mark your answers in column a or b.
- Add up each vertical column.
- The totals in the shaded boxes are your scores for each face.

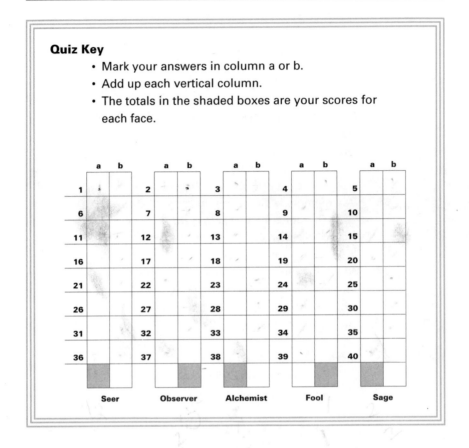

	a	b		a	b		a	b		a	b		a	b
1			**2**			**3**			**4**			**5**		
6			**7**			**8**			**9**			**10**		
11			**12**			**13**			**14**			**15**		
16			**17**			**18**			**19**			**20**		
21			**22**			**23**			**24**			**25**		
26			**27**			**28**			**29**			**30**		
31			**32**			**33**			**34**			**35**		
36			**37**			**38**			**39**			**40**		
Seer			**Observer**			**Alchemist**			**Fool**			**Sage**		

Building Your Creative Profile

Before you move ahead to examine each of the Five Faces in depth and learn the skills associated with each one, it's important to take note of where your own strengths and weaknesses currently lie. Your highest score in the shaded boxes of the test key above is your primary creative style, and your lowest score in the shaded boxes is your least developed creative style. Write the names of the two Faces in which you scored highest on lines 1 and 2 under Dominant Faces. You may have scored equally on some or all of the Faces. That's fine, too. It means that you are already balancing these skills. In that case, choose two of the Faces that most appeal to you. These will act as your Dominant Faces, which you can focus on improving. Write the name of the Face on which you scored the lower on line 3 below. This is your Growth Opportunity—the place where you can make the most improvement. Again, if you scored equally, choose one you would particularly like to strengthen.

Dominant Faces (highest scores)

1. _____

2. _____

Growth Opportunity Face (lowest score)

3. _____

This quiz reflects a first step in understanding your creative style. Once you've studied all the Faces, you can work on mastering them as a portfolio of skills.

You may be surprised by the scores from the quiz. Don't let this discourage you. This may be the first time you've been exposed to thinking about how you create ideas. As you read through the Faces chapters, you'll have a better understanding of how you can improve the entire range of your imagination.

Your goal is to master all Five Faces of Genius. So while you may be dominant in one particular Face, you'll want to learn how to add the other four creative tools to your toolbox. Highly creative folks have all the Faces at their disposal, and you can, too.

Read through the following five chapters about the Faces of Genius and you'll grow to understand the power of each skill and the unique gifts you can bring to your creative enterprises. You'll find exercises designed to teach you how to use them when faced with various types of business situations, whether they be new product development, customer service, marketing, sales, competitive insight, or brand positioning. You will learn how bringing a deeper imagination to your life and work can make you a more effective, efficient, and fulfilled manager. You'll also learn how you can bring these skills into play among teams in the workplace.

Right now you might feel as if your imagination is terra incognita, or uncharted territory. In the business renaissance, our mission is similar to the ancient explorers'—to navigate undiscovered territory. Once you understand your imagination, you can bring your genius to work. We no longer manage only the business in front of us, but we create the undiscovered business of the future. Let the Five Faces of Genius lead you into the future.

1. THE SEER

THE POWER TO IMAGE

I shut my eyes in order that I may see.
—PAUL GAUGUIN

Ray Kroc is the business genius who created the McDonald's restaurant empire. As a milkshake mixer salesman, he visited the then-family-owned McDonald's restaurant in San Bernardino, California. The quick service, quality food, and low prices filled his mind with possibilities. "That night in my motel room I did a lot of heavy thinking about what I'd seen during the day. Visions of McDonald's restaurants dotting crossroads all over the country paraded through my brain." The pictures marching through Kroc's head were the beginnings of the McDonald's franchise. Kroc could have decided to merely franchise one or two stores, but in his mind's eye he saw the future—pictures of restaurants all over the nation and the world. Here is an example of a highly developed Seer.

The first principle of the *Five Faces of Genius* is the Seer—the power to image, or visualize. Seers "see" pictures in their mind's eye. These visual images are the impetus for ingenious ideas. Mastering this power is the first step to mastering your imagination.

You may not be conscious of it, but you use this power to visualize every day. You imagine how you would look driving the sports car of your dreams down a winding country road. As you play catch with your son, you see how he will look suited up for his first Little League game. The only difference between you and a creative genius is that he uses these mental images to generate new ideas. Whether these images are snapshots of products yet to be designed, mental "movies" of employees' working more productively after new management decisions are implemented, or symbolic pictures, such as charts or graphs, highly creative people honor their pictures, study them, and use them to create ideas. The pictures in their mind's eye lead them into new frontiers.

Seers use a three-pronged approach to creative thinking:

1. **Seers pay attention to the images in their mind's eye.**
2. **Seers allow themselves to visualize in great detail.**
3. **Seers manipulate their images to discover great ideas.**

In this section, you will see how artists and scientists have used their Seer skills to create. Then you will learn how you can use the same skills successfully in the workplace.

The Creative Genius of the Seer: To See the Future, Shut Your Eyes

Most know the artist Georgia O'Keeffe by her colorful, abstract paintings of flowers and bones. But did you know that her training was in a representational style? In fact, she won an award at the Art Institute of Chicago for a traditional still-life painting called "Dead Rabbit by a Copper Pot." It featured a dead rabbit by a copper pot.

As O'Keeffe matured she decided to forget her training and paint the images in her mind's eye. She laid down her colors, grabbed her charcoal, and began drawing on paper that covered the floor. She said, "I have things in my head that are not like what anyone has taught me—shapes and ideas so near to me, so natural to my way of being and thinking, that it hadn't occurred to me to put them down."

The things she saw in her head were abstract images. These lines and shapes formed the pictures that ultimately defined her as the mother of American modern art. Having the courage to draw what she saw in her mind's eye was the genius moment that moved her painting from status quo to breakthrough. She saw the future of painting by shutting her eyes.

SEERS PAY ATTENTION TO THE PICTURES IN THEIR MIND'S EYE

The pictures in their heads fascinate Seers and lead them toward a new future. Each image becomes a beacon on the horizon that keeps the artist moving ahead. Some even say the picture has a life of its own, as if the picture always existed and the artist is only seeing it for the first time. The image *is* the wisdom. Seers honor the pictures in their imagination.

For Einstein, the theory of relativity began as an image. Since his youth, Einstein pondered the picture of someone riding on a wave of light. What would the landscape look like as the person traveled through space? "He wondered how things would look to him if he rode on a light beam. He glanced back at Bern's clock tower while riding a streetcar and thought, What if the streetcars were moving at the speed of light? Applying his new theory, he decided that the clock would appear to him to have stopped, while the watch in his pocket would continue to run at its usual rate. This confirmed his idea that time is not the same for all observers when objects approach the speed of light." Einstein paid attention to his image. Pondered it. Cherished it. Trusted that it had some wisdom to offer. His genius breakthrough came when he allowed himself to stay obsessed with the image of traveling at the speed of light.

You can often tell Seers because an image may appear so strongly to them that they can't think about anything else. When Seers have these visions, they pay attention to them until they are sure they have fully fleshed them out. It's almost as if the pictures have them by the neck and they have no choice but to explore them. Consider the writer Robertson Davies's description of his inspirational moments: "An idea for a novel seizes me and will not let me go. What often appears in my head is a picture which somehow must be considered." Davies was visited with an image of a boy throwing a snowball, and that picture kicks off the story line for his novel *The Fifth Business*.

While we cannot always will these "flashes of brilliance," we can become more aware of them. Most of us "see" many images in our mind's eye every day, but we blow them off or don't make the time to consider them. However, when we start to value these pictures, we begin to find fodder for greater ideas. This is what distinguishes the creative person—*the expectation that the images contain an idea worthy of pursuit.* Leonardo da Vinci said, "Whatever exists in the universe, in essence, in appearance, in the imagination, the painter has first in his mind and then in his hands." To see the future, shut your eyes.

SEERS VISUALIZE IN GREAT DETAIL

The ability to visualize in detail is at the heart of the Seers' skills. Once they have a picture in their mind, they can describe the image as precisely as if they were reading the statistics off the back of a baseball card. They can see the nuances of the picture, describe the scene, and narrate the small things. Remember the movie *Amadeus*? Toward the end of the film, Salieri, the court composer, poses as the grim reaper and plans Mozart's demise. As Mozart lies dying, Salieri forces Mozart to write his final symphony. Mozart dictates to Salieri the musical score he sees in his mind's eye.

> MOZART: Start with the voices. Basses first. Second beat of the first measure—A. (singing the note) Con-fu-ta-tis. (speaking) Second measure, second beat. (singing) Ma-le-dic-tis. (speaking) G-sharp, of course.
>
> SALIERI: Yes.
>
> MOZART: Third measure, second beat starting on E. (singing) Flam-mis a-cri-bus ad-dic-tis. (speaking) And fourth measure, fourth beat—D. (singing) Ma-le-dic-tis, flam-mis a-cri-bus ad-dic-tis. (speaking) Do you have that?
>
> SALIERI: I think so.
>
> MOZART: Sing it back.
>
> [Salieri sings back the first six measures of the bass line. After the first two measures a chorus of basses fades in on the soundtrack and engulfs his voice. They stop.]
>
> MOZART: Good. Now the tenors. Fourth beat of the first measure—C. (singing) Con-fu-ta-tis. (speaking) Second measure, fourth beat on D. (singing) Ma-le-dic-tis. (speaking) All right?
>
> SALIERI: Yes.

Salieri frantically copies down the manna from heaven. Mozart is simply describing the detailed music score—the notes, timing, and orchestration—from the image he sees in his mind's eye.

Earlier I shared how Mozart understood his Seer moments. He said, "My subject . . . stands almost complete and finished in my mind, so that I survey it like a fine picture or a beautiful statue, at a glance." Did you catch that? Scores of music—surveyed at a glance. Seers take the time to appreciate the detail their mental images have to offer. While holding an image in their mind, Seers analyze its landscape and find fresh ideas.

SEERS MANIPULATE IMAGES TO DISCOVER GREAT IDEAS

Seers intentionally alter the images they see to test new ideas. They morph ideas and try to evolve new outcomes. When Seers become confident, they are able to mold their mental pictures like Play-Doh to see what they can come up with.

The Nobel Prize–winning physicist Richard Feynman had remarkable intuition. He saw mathematical calculations in his mind's eye. From flying function signs to floating colored variables, he manipulated formulas in his imagination. It is said of Feynman's study of Euclidean geometry problems: "He manipulated the diagrams in his mind; he anchored some points and let others float, imagined some lines as stiff rods and others as stretchable bands, and let the shapes slide until he could see what the result must be." Like rearranging furniture in his mind, he experimented with new configurations. The manipulation of the images led to his insights.

When I heard the film director Sidney Lumet talk about his creative process, I was surprised to hear him articulate this Seer skill. He says he develops "mini-movies" in his head. By reordering and changing the scenes in the movie, he sparks unconventional solutions and finds the most inventive way to tell his story.

Now that you have a clear picture of how the Seer skills lead to breakthrough ideas in the arts and sciences, let's examine how the same skills are responsible for some of the most successful business breakthroughs of history.

Mastering the Seer at Work

Some of the most inventive minds in business are Seers. As you'll see, for business geniuses visualization is a highly developed tool in the arsenal of creative enterprise. From envisioning better ways to communicate with colleagues to creating a mission statement for your company, you can take on the skills of the Seer to discover new ideas and move from status quo to breakthrough. Now that you have learned the three-part approach of the Seer, I'm going to introduce you to specific ways you can apply them to begin to realize your creative potential.

IMAGE THE BUSINESS FUTURE

Seers use their power with pictures to create a plethora of possible business solutions and to predict the uncharted territory of their company and industry.

Delia's is a clothing company with a vision. They target Generation Y girls ages twelve to seventeen and provide them with the clothing they crave—inexpensive T-shirts, trendy jeans, lots of cool accessories. Their prices are affordable and their fashion is unbeatable. When the company founders talk about the future of Delia's, you hear the Seer at work. They visualize a future in which Delia's is an essential part of every teenage girl's life. Founder Stephen Kahn says, "We are going to own this generation." Delia's wants to be the company that meets a generation's needs throughout the span of their lives. They define the company not by what they sell today, but by the future in the mind's eye.

You've worked with Seers before. When they talk about their ideas, they say, "It looks like this . . ." or "Can you see it?" and they go on to describe a picture of what they see in their head. You can also identify the Seers in your office because they like to close their eyes. Have you ever been sitting in a conference room, working on a problem, and a colleague has his eyes shut? He's not taking a nap. He's thinking hard, waiting for a picture that might be the impetus for a new idea.

Robert was a client who couldn't talk without a pencil in his hand. He would grab a pad or turn over a memo and start to draw his images. From flow charts to organic-shaped renderings, Robert would sketch his ideas.

As I watched, I realized he was practiced at the skills of a Seer. He paid attention to his visions, imagined them in great detail, and manipulated those visions to develop creative business ideas. The paper and pencil were just an extention of his brain.

When you begin to pay attention to the images you have in your mind's eye, you'll see creative solutions for your own business and work. You'll be in the shower and you'll visualize a new service to offer your clients. You'll put your head on your pillow and see a new way to work with a colleague. You'll be commuting on the train and have a picture pop into your head of how to help a new customer.

In a business world characterized by change, you can divine the next trend using the skill of the Seer. You can learn to be an idea generator rather than a follower. Look around and assess the leaders you know. They are the ones who use their Seer skills to create the new thing, the next thing, the next trend before others. Your Seer skills can accelerate your powers of prediction and land you in the future.

Wayne Huizinga, the business mogul who created Blockbuster Video and Waste Management, is reinventing yet another market—purchasing cars. He predicted customers would become increasingly frustrated with the time-consuming and anxiety-producing process of buying a car and would demand new ways to shop. He imagined a place called Auto-Nation, where people would go for no-haggle car shopping. The sticker price is the only price. You don't have to strike a deal with a sales agent and there are money-back guarantees—things traditional dealerships don't offer. Huizinga found something that needed fixing and pictured the future.

Try these simple imaging exercises:

1. To become more familiar with your Seer skills, make a practice of closing your eyes at work.

Allow yourself to daydream about possible solutions to a business problem. Some people find this simple action has great creative rewards. Try it. When you're in a meeting that demands creative solutions, when you're talking on the phone trying to solve a problem, or when you're trying to describe an idea to a friend or colleague. It's easier to visualize when your eyes are closed. Practice using your inner eye. What images do you see? What ideas do they generate? Don't forget to let yourself dwell on these images. You'll find they will improve your world.

2. Ask yourself, "What is the wildly successful picture?"

If I was to see a picture of the ideal outcome for my company and for myself, what would it look like? Creative solutions come from thinking big while knowing the landscape of limitations. Which are solid limitations that can't be moved? Which are soft and malleable? When you picture the wildly successful outcome, you call the barriers into question and see new possibilities. This is a way you can use your Seer skills to break through the barriers and imagine the future.

BE A MISSION MAKER

Seers are often the mission makers—the goal setters of the organization. By using the images in their mind's eye, they become the leaders who create the future project, the future department, the future company. As one client who works for a major entertainment firm says, he can "see the finish line."

Pleasant Rowland is the founder and president of the Pleasant Company, a firm that sells high-quality dolls with a unique spin. Each doll tells a story of courage and adventure based on American history. From books to Broadway musicals, Rowland has crafted a unique life experience for girls to learn about their country's heritage. If you haven't visited their retail store, the American Girl Place, in Chicago, you're missing one of the most brilliant business breakthroughs of the twenty-first century.

When Rowland began the company, she talked to an investment banker about the picture in her mind's eye. She told of her vision to manufacture unique dolls, sell them via direct mail, and create special events for girls to experience stories of courage. But the banker questioned her focus. A start-up company could never succeed in these diverse industries. Rowland told the banker that she wasn't in the manufacturing or marketing business. She said, "We are in the girl business." She had a picture in her mind's eye of the young girl she wanted to serve. Recently purchased by Mattel, for $700 million, the Pleasant Company is an example of breakthrough born by visualizing a mission. She saw a young girl at the finish line.

You might be wondering how you can be a mission maker when you are not the CEO of the company. While you may not be responsible for writing the mission statement for the entire company, you *can* decide what you do every day and the part you play in the larger company. Imagine a picture of your goal in your mind's eye. Do you want to start a new project? Serve another type of customer? Do you see a new way to make money? Challenge yourself to see an image that both intrigues you *and* satisfies the needs of the firm. Use your power to imagine and become a mission maker for yourself.

Scott was a writer for the lifestyle section of a popular magazine. After a few years, he found his creative energy dwindling in his work. He wasn't as interested in lifestyle topics as much as he used to be. I encouraged him to visualize what stories he would *like* to cover that would tap his creative passion. He saw himself in his study, poring over his biographies of scientists and books about biotechnology. He saw himself at his computer writing about the sciences he loved. He believed there was an audience for "light" science that no magazine had yet tapped, and he decided to approach his boss about including an accessible science segment.

To his surprise and delight, Scott was given the green light to write a weekly feature called "Science You Can Use," which surveyed popular trends in science. In fact, the management at the magazine was looking for a fresh approach that would attract new readers. Scott said, "I never imagined my personal mission could find a home in my company's corporate mission. I know my mission will change again and again as I progress. But today I can find my creative spirit at this company." Scott found the intersection between his interests and the interests of the firm by becaming a mission maker.

Mission makers are not just CEOs. This may be hard to believe, but in a business renaissance the folks closest to the sale of the product or service have increased power and influence. People on the sales floor, bank tellers, and customer service people often have the best information about what is happening in a changing market. And because they have the best information, they can create the best ideas. When folks on the front lines visualize making things better for themselves *and* the company, they create breakthrough ideas and find their business genius.

Leo, a customer service representative of a regional phone company, had a small business client who wanted to set up a voice-mail system. By the time the client had finally navigated his way through the phone company to find Leo, he was already frustrated. The voice-mail options the client wanted were not offered by the phone company. Yet Leo had a hunch that the technological capabilities the client needed existed within the firm. So rather than tell the client the phone company couldn't deliver, Leo said he would investigate the request and call the client back with an answer.

Leo said, "I had a picture in my mind's eye that guided me through this customer's problem. I saw my hand reaching across the wires to link with a customer's hand and offer support. I was frustrated that I couldn't provide what this customer needed, so I decided to press on within our behemoth company to see what I could do. My image inspired me to try harder."

After some internal wrangling, Leo found a way to configure the voice-mail connection that satisfied his customer. Now the service is provided for all small-business clients. Leo's image of being a helping hand directed the work toward the solution. "Without the image of myself as a helping hand across the miles, I wouldn't have cared enough at that moment to try."

Here are some ways to begin to make a mission for yourself at work using the Seer skills:

1. Visualize a job bigger than your own.

Try to see a picture of a job you would like to tackle. Fight to see an image in your mind's eye. What do *you* want to accomplish? This job may not yet exist, but use you Seer skills to dream up a mission. Visualize yourself as group manager, team leader, or even CEO. How would you solve the problems your firm faces? The image may lead you to an inventive mission for yourself. Genius business ideas come when we open up the vista of our responsibilities.

2. Share what you see in your mind's eye.

Most of us have the power to image, but we are hesitant to share our images. We don't want to be perceived as weird or less-than-linear types. However, business intuition can be powerful. Remember how much your company needs a business artist. Share the ideas you have for your firm's mission. Clearly describe the vision in your mind's eye. Say things like, "I see a solution that looks like this . . ." This is how you become the mission maker both for you and others.

VISUALIZE UNMET NEEDS

With almost X-ray vision, Seers use their ability to image and mine details to determine the unmet needs of their colleagues, their individual customers, and the general market of their products and services. By visualizing their market in different ways, they discover ways to meet their needs. Customers are rarely aware of all the ways you or your firm can help them. Seers use pictures in their mind's eye to figure out what others want even before they recognize it themselves. They unearth the inarticulate.

Consider 3Com's introduction of a personal digital assistant called the Palm V. The design team recognized an unmet need behind these hand-held computers that surprised them. They assumed people purchased PalmPilots to communicate with the office quickly, to download e-mail, and to hold addresses and phone numbers. But they imagined an even deeper need—status. They imagined people thinking "I'm cool if I have a Palm Pilot. I get attention" and they designed accordingly. They made the computer sleek, sexy, and even mimicked the product numbers of the BMW 3, 5, 7 series. Digging for the unmet need revealed something no one else had addressed—the need to be cool—and 3Com exploited it to create a business breakthrough.

You can use your power to imagine what is really happening below the surface. Once you have a picture in your mind, focus on the details. What are the small influences? What is missing from this picture? If these people could unabashedly ask for what they needed, what would they say?

Visualize what unmet needs exist within your job responsibilities. Perhaps your cranky co-workers need to feel included. Perhaps your angry customer needs to feel cared for. Perhaps your reluctant client needs to shine in front his management. When you start visualizing what's going on under the surface, you find wholly different ideas.

Don't forget that new ideas often come with a flash of intuition. Don't push your mental pictures to the side because you are busy. Often a new product or service is born just by waking up to those very pictures. An inventor at Procter & Gamble found his inspiration for leak guards in diapers in just this way. "I was picturing my arm as a baby's leg. I started playing with my sweater and tucked the edge of the cuff under." This mental image was the spark for the creation of a brilliant innovation in Pampers diapers. Meeting an unmet need through the power of visualization.

Take the first step to discovering the unmet needs of your business:

1. Practice visualizing a customer experience between yourself and your firm.

Make a habit of imagining what it is like to do business with your firm. What is it like to be on the receiving end of your service? Ordering products, asking for help, being in another department? What do those images look like? Strive to re-create the experience as a picture in your mind's eye. As you practice, ask yourself, "What are the unmet needs?" Expect great ideas.

2. Picture a scenario in your mind's eye of what may happen to your customers and clients in the year ahead.

What trends do you sense around you? How might the world be changing? What's the next thing? What do you see? Then visualize the role you'd like to play in the future. How do you see yourself meeting the changing needs? What potential services could your firm offer? How could you change your job description in the changing climate? When a picture enters your head, allow yourself to dwell on it and flesh it out. Let it grow and develop—use a pen and paper if you want to sketch your ideas. Visualize tomorrow's unmet needs today.

SEE STEPPING-STONES

Skilled Seers in business know it's not enough to see the need or the ultimate goal—you need to know what steps to take in order to meet it. Just as the director Sidney Lumet makes mini-movies in his mind, the business artist manipulates the sequence of the images to create clear steps to the future. When you have some confidence in your Seer skills, you can practice seeing the stepping-stones to get to your wildly successful visions.

Let's examine how Nordstrom management does this. Before Nordstrom designs a building, they create a mini-movie of the experience of a customer as she walks through the store. They envision lots of space in the aisles—enough room to roam and linger. They see the customer sitting near a piano, enjoying music. They see customers having lunch together.

The endgame is that Nordstrom's management never wants a customer to leave the store and enter the mall. They have imagined the stepping-stones needed to accomplish their vision. From one picture to the next, Nordstrom scripts a customer experience in which everything that is needed is within their four walls.

Just as an engineer might see different possible paths for the circuitry configuration on a motherboard, so the Seer in business can manipulate their pictures and come up with a variety of options as to how to achieve their business objectives. They try to see more than one set of steps.

Owens Corning was dying in the 1980s. Famous for using the Pink Panther to promote PINK Fiberglas insulation, the firm didn't stand for much more. Turning it around required a creative image. Owens Corning saw a new place to compete in the trend toward home improvement. They redefined their business scope as a picture that they called the "shell of the house." They began to survey potential companies to buy that would help them achieve their final vision. By purchasing a window pane company and a siding firm, among others, Owens Corning redesigned to deliver the "shell of the house" services for their customers. They used this power to image multiple options or stepping-stones to get to the vision.

Seeing the stepping-stones lets you break apart the problem to find the fertile linkage points that can help you move from one spot to the next. Developing your Seer skills will help you visualize the baby steps that lead to big solutions.

To begin to master the stepping-stones of the Seer, try this exercise:

1. Practice using your eye as a photographer's lens.

What would be the key photos in a picture album of your success? Consider mentally "framing" shots you might photograph to chronicle the changes it would take to get to your vision.

2. Map out a project like a mini-movie.

Image the final outcome of your project—that will be your last scene of the movie. Then create the supporting scenes that lead to the middle and the end. Fight to see pictures. These "mini-scenes" can lead you to breakthrough solutions for your project.

Here is a summary of the key business principles of the Seer:

1. Image the business future: Visualize new opportunities and
    potential outcomes.
2. Be a mission maker: Picture the end goal for yourself at work.
3. Visualize unmet needs: See the underlying needs you can
    meet.
4. See stepping-stones: Imagine the steps to accomplish your
    vision.

Seers and Teams

Because Seers frequently use pictures to convey concepts, they are typically good at designing the future of the business. They can visualize possible ideas for the team to consider and give detailed descriptions of the solutions. Seers can be the eyes of a team's vision. Let's say your team decides to talk to a client about increasing the firm's charges. A Seer may say, "I can see what the client's objections will be right now. Let's tackle each one separately so we are prepared to give her a thorough response." Seers use the picture of the outcome to tackle the present challenge. They share their images freely with the team. They are often the inspiration the team needs to go forward.

A dominant Seer describes how she runs meetings: "I always like to use the image in my mind's eye as a starting place for the discussion." For example, when she brought her team together to discuss how to work together more effectively across departments, she kicked the meeting off like this: "My vision is that at the end of this meeting, we will walk out of here understanding what each person needs to work together better. I'd like to see our communication over the next three months improve. I can envision we'll be laughing one day that we had these issues." She, in effect, creates a mini-movie that describes the objectives of the time together and what she wants the midterm goal and the final outcome to be.

Teams tend to rely on and trust the creative vision of the Seer. The Seer's forward stance to ideas is refreshing and well accepted. Their visions are valuable and it's helpful to have two or more folks in the group who can use Seer skills. When you do, you can spread the responsibility for ideas around and raise the quantity of ideas generated.

Teams also use Seers as reality checks for the group's ideas and inspirations. Seers encourage others to think through the details of ideas and sequencing of events. They'll ask clarifying questions: "How do we see this idea working?"; "What might the solutions look like?" They may even begin to narrate the group's idea or talk about their stepping-stone vision for it. If a Seer can't create a picture that "works" from the idea that is under construction, then the idea may not be worth pursuing.

Business disciplines traditionally considered "creative" are full of Seers. Communications, public relations, advertising, and design attract those with skills of creative visualization. But other less obvious careers attract Seers as well—attorneys, information technology engineers, and operations and sales people. Business areas where Seers should be especially valued are ones in which logistical problems must be thought through, or process and systems areas where manipulation and alteration of the flow of information is required.

A SEER TEAM EXERCISE

When your team begins a challenge, ask each person to describe a picture of their wildly successful outcome. If you were to meet the challenge in the best way possible, what might it look like? Let each person paint a verbal picture. Illustrate the rich image in the mind's eye. Talk about the detail you see.

Next choose a vision that most closely represents the consensus of the group. You may need to manipulate or adjust the vision, but agree to focus on one. Then begin to construct stepping-stones. How might you get there? What would be the first steps? The midterm steps? Use the power of the group to manipulate the picture together. Try drawings or sketch the team's ideas together. These techniques will help to focus the group's imagination and navigate you toward new solutions.

Seer Pitfalls to Avoid

Because Seers begin using their power to image early in life, they can over-rely on it as a creative skill. Each of us leans on our dominant Face of

Genius, but it's especially hard for the Seer to branch out. They get great ideas from visualization, but they tend to rely on it to the exclusion of the other skills. More than any other face, Seers need to work hard to expand their portfolio of tools.

Seers should learn to combine their images with the skills of others in the group. For instance, the power to image combined with the Observer, whom you'll meet in a moment, produces a business artist who notices detail, draws conclusions about what the detail means, and then visualizes a creative idea. Seers can bring business genius to teams when they synthesize their skills with others.

Seers must learn to share their visions openly. Strong Seers are sometimes unaware of all the moments they use their skills. The ability to visualize is at times an unconscious process but until Seers talk openly about the power of pictures, they won't realize their full idea potential. For some, becoming a better Seer means only becoming aware of what you already do *and* trying to do it in the presence of others.

The Five Faces of Genius Summary

	THE SEER	THE OBSERVER	THE ALCHEMIST	THE FOOL	THE SAGE
The Creative Power Principle	The Power to Image	The Power to Notice Detail	The Power to Connect Domains	The Power to Celebrate Weakness	The Power to Simplify
Key Creative Skill	Visualization				
Easy Way to Remember the Face	See it				
Benefit to Teams	Vision for future Test possible outcomes				
Pitfalls	Needs to combine Seer with other Faces				

Exercises

Now that you have a good idea of how the Seer skills work, try these more advanced exercises using all the steps of the Seer. (Refer to the chart above.)

1. A Nordstrom salesperson said he "sees" the sales floor like Larry Bird "sees" the basketball court. The salesperson scopes out new customers and directs them to the right merchandise. The salesperson organizes the items on the floor and arranges them in the most attractive way possible—all toward the "goal" of getting customers to the register. Imagine that your business is a basketball court. Try to see a picture in your mind's eye. Envision the important activities going on. These activities can be new-product introductions, customer problems, profitability concerns, or some others. What movements do you "see" on the court? Visualize the scene and describe it below.

_____

_____

_____

_____

_____

_____

_____

Imagine that you are a creative offensive player, like Michael Jordan. How do you maximize the opportunities you see on the basketball court?

_____

_____

_____

_____

_____

_____

_____

2. Imagine that you are offered a ride on Aladdin's magic carpet. The carpet transports you one year into the future. The carpet shows you the view of your entire business year. You see it transpire in one long swoop. What do you see from high in the sky? What happened in the business that you expected? What surprised you? What happened that you didn't anticipate? Describe below what you see in your mind's eye.

_____

_____

_____

_____

_____

_____

_____

3. Imagine in your mind's eye that you are watching the board-room of your biggest competitor through a surveillance camera. During the meeting, the group reveals its plan for the coming year. Describe what you see and hear below.

_____

_____

_____

_____

_____

_____

_____

Lying Down on the Job

One day at work I had my feet up on the desk and my eyes closed. I was trying to solve a client problem that had dogged my team for weeks. Because I'm a primarily a Seer, I was fighting to see alternative pictures in my mind's eye. I wondered how to make the problem work.

My boss happened by. He stepped into my office and announced that if I wanted to take a nap, I should close my door. He obviously thought I was sleeping. And the message was, in this culture, napping isn't accepted.

You'll be happy to know that times are changing. It's becoming widely recognized by corporations that napping energizes and renews employees. Some firms are installing napping centers. Some even have tents and head sets available for napping. The thought is that once you've recharged you will have surplus energy reserves that make for creative enterprise.

Here are some thoughts on napping at work designed to give you the courage to try it.

1. Lie down often.

Mihaly Csikszentmihalyi, the University of Chicago professor who has spent years researching creativity, says, "Creative persons often take rests and sleep a lot . . . their energy is under their control—it is not controlled by the calendar, the clock, an external schedule. When necessary, they can focus it like a laser."

Part of the reason a business manager's creative energy is not under control is that we are too tired. We come to work tired and ignore our energy barometers. We leave work tired, only to repeat the same cycle the next day.

Your creative energy can be more easily regulated if you find a way to respect when it's low. Learn to take rests. Develop ingenious ways to nap.

2. Keep an air mattress in your work area.

In our workshops we give each person an air mattress. They keep the mattress behind their door or in their cubicle. When they need a rest, they can pull it out and lie down.

Many business professionals have couches in their offices. Make your "couch" from an air mattress. This practice may cause a stir, but it will certainly increase your creative reputation!

3. Lie down to think.

Common business practice is to sit in a chair while thinking, yet some of our best thinking happens when we lie down. Think about it—when you're falling asleep; while you are reclining in your car as a passenger; before you get out of bed. More oxygen to the brain increases your surplus energy level and your creativity quotient.

When I first met the CEO of a company for whom I worked, he was conducting a meeting lying down on the boardroom table. I couldn't believe it. Yet he set the example that lying down is part of the creative life of the company.

Some of my best creative work happens in a colleague's office when I lie down on the floor while she and another colleague and I work. The extra oxygen to my brain coupled with the new perspective from the floor always gives me a boost of brilliance.

4. Find solitude during work.

Try to protect your alone time. Don't fill your schedule to overflowing with meetings. Don't become seduced by busyness. Remember: You are in a business renaissance—an economy that values ideas. In the end, you are as valuable as your ideas. Don't substitute meetings for the harder work of personal invention.

If you don't practice struggling for ideas alone, you're not going to know how to master *your* business imagination. You won't have an imagination that your company can "rent."

5. Begin a "closed-door policy."

Shut your door regularly. Put up a "Do Not Disturb" sign. Use your time for reflection, solution finding, business artist time. Think. It's the best part of the job. And that's what any employer is paying you to do.

Don't have a door to close? Go to a coffee shop. Book a conference room for yourself. Stay home and work. As one business artist of a leading company told her staff, "I don't care where you go to work. Just come *here* with ideas."

6. Schedule inspiration transitions.

Most ideas happen at the transition between focused energy and relaxation. That's the sandwich time between working hard and kicking back. Be sure to build intervals of relaxation into your day. Wait for inspiration in those periods. Try to have a journal on hand to record your ideas. (For more on business journaling, see page 88.) These are the breaks when your business muse will speak. Pay attention.

Some business artists do this by planning business "excursions." These are frequent trips to be out in the action—walking the store floor, roaming the halls, interacting with colleagues, or going out just to be with customers. Make friends with these places of business. Find places to relax even in the thick of your business day. You will find the best ideas come when you are *not* focusing directly on the problem.

How the Seer Helps You Discover Business Insights

Seers use their visual skill to discover insights. They "see" the real motivation, the barriers, the inner nature of a situation. Like Superman with X-ray vision, Seers see what's truly going on.

The actor Sean Penn called insight "uncommon thoughts about common matters." Thinking uncommon thoughts is the vortex of innovation. Penn said that to do this you have to "break through your conditioning and see what doesn't apply."

A business insight is an uncommon thought about a common business situation. It is discovering the hidden "reasons why" of what happens at work, seeing the inner nature of the business, breaking through your conditioning—the sacred rules of business. It is using intuition and bringing it to bear on your challenges.

Consider General Mills, the makers of Yoplait yogurt. They found kids loved yogurt but rarely ate it. Kids might have yogurt for breakfast or after school, but almost never for lunch. They wondered why moms didn't pack yogurt cups in lunches.

The Yoplait team had an insight. *Moms don't want to pack spoons to eat the yogurt.* Spoons are bad news. Kids lose them. They waste money. So Yoplait developed a plastic tube packaging called Go-Gurts, portable yogurt that's easy to pack in any lunch. When Go-Gurts launched, they were so popular grocers couldn't keep enough on the shelves. General Mills realized the hidden reason—the inner nature of the problem—and then devised an inventive solution.

An insight is not a fact. It is an assumption, a hunch, or an intuition about a fact. It means you guess why things are the way they are.

An insight gives you more to work with—ideas on how you might counteract the problem.

Here are some ways the Seer skills help you become more insightful in your work.

1. Shut your eyes to "facts" and listen to your intuition.

We like to base our ideas on fact. We want to be sure of our information before we create a solution.

But facts are rarely as watertight as we think. It's the *value* we assign to the fact that drives the kinds of ideas we create. Give more value to your hunches, your intuitions, your inklings of what might be true. You can always use the facts later to check your ideas. You'll find more business genius when you lead with your intuition.

2. Grow intuition antennae.

Insects use their antennae to navigate. They can't see well, so they put out their feelers and sense for information to guide them.

Use your "sense" of what's going on to guide you. Business folks are slow to trust their intuition, yet we are often right. We are the first to know when there is a problem or opportunity, but fail to act because we're fearful we don't have enough information. Try to image the potential influences, why things might be as they are. Let your antennae guide you.

3. Image yourself in the situation.

Try to visualize how you would think and feel if you personally were encountering the business situation. Like in the Yoplait example, ask yourself why you wouldn't want to pack a lunch with yogurt.

Personal experience is the ingredient we use to make ideas. Intuitions are always conditioned by our experience. Practice going with it. It's all any genius has got.

4. Share your visions with others.

You can't always prove intuitions but they are the grist of great big ideas. Insights based on "intuitive knowing" don't always make you feel sure of your recommendations. All you have is an instinct. Share it anyway.

I have a young colleague who joined a public relations firm in an entry-level position. In a brainstorming session with the president of the company, he had an idea to share but felt as a newcomer he should keep his idea to himself. Sometime later in the brainstorming session someone else shared the exact idea he had. The team had great enthusiasm for the concept. He kicked himself for censoring his intuition. Haven't we all been in that situation? The lesson: Share your intuitions.

5. Make sure your insight isn't just a fact.

Some business folks are so eager for an insight, they learn something new and call the learning an insight. Remember insights are *uncommon* thoughts about common situations. Ask yourself, "How uncommon is this interpretation? Am I really seeing this in a fresh way? Or is it a fact in disguise."

6. Use all the Five Faces of Genius skills.

Seers use their power with pictures to discover insights. But as you'll see, all the Faces also offer roads to navigating insights. Master them all.

2. THE OBSERVER

THE POWER TO NOTICE DETAIL

"The poet's eye, in a fine frenzy rolling,
Doth glance from heaven to earth, from earth to heaven."
—WILLIAM SHAKESPEARE

Walt Disney put his daughter on a playground carousel. His Observer skills kicked into high gear and the idea for a family theme park was born. Disney wondered why there couldn't be a park where adults and kids could play together. His biographer said this, "As his daughter went on the rides, Walt studied the boredom of other parents, and he noted the squalor of the park—paint cracking on the carousel horse, the ground dirty and littered, the ride operators cheerless and unfriendly." Disney noticed the details and they became the yeast for his theme park idea—now the finest in family entertainment. By paying attention to the details of our experience, breakthroughs are born.

The second principle of the Five Faces of Genius is the ability to stand in awe of the world, notice small things, and make creative contributions from the details. The Observer collects a basket of information and then makes some radiant interpretation from its content.

You can increase your ability to find breakthrough ideas in your life and work by trying on the skills of the Observer. But first let's explore how the

Observer's creative genius works. Observers' skills are evidenced in four key ways:

1. Observers stand in awe of the world around them.
2. Observers notice and cherish detail.
3. Observers are driven by their unrelenting curiosity.
4. Observers use beauty as the inspiration for ideas.

The Creative Genius of the Observer: Make Big Ideas from Small Ingredients

Robert Frost's first published poem was called "My Butterfly." His genius moment for the poem came while he was walking through the woods and observing. With head down, he surveyed the forest floor. Among the fallen leaves he noticed a dead butterfly. He picked it up, became entranced, and found the inspiration for this poem.

> *And there were other things:*
> *It seemed God let thee flutter from His gentle clasp:*
> *Then fearful He had let thee win*
> *Too far beyond Him to be gathered in,*
> *Snatched thee, o'ereager, with ungentle grasp.*
> . . . .
>
> *I found that wing broken today!*
> *For thou art dead, I said,*
> *And the strange birds say.*
> *I found it with the withered leaves*
> *Under the eaves.*

This power to notice detail and find inspiration from it is the creative genius of the Observer. The Observer's curiosity is like a radar constantly scanning the environment, looking for small things that lead to big ideas. When you find the Observer within you, you will discover that you can meet genius ideas in the most common places.

OBSERVERS STAND IN AWE OF THE WORLD

Observers are awestruck by the world around them: the movement of the clouds at sunset, the expression of a pained face, the smell of needles from an evergreen tree. Observers pay attention to things that may seem insignificant at first, to others and even to themselves, but upon reflection contain tremendous creative rewards.

To get a better handle on the skills of the Observer, it's helpful to think about the inspiration process of writers. Writers are familiar with the benefits of observing details. The great Southern novelist Eudora Welty tells us how observation inspired her calling as an author.

"At around age six perhaps I was standing by myself in our front yard waiting for supper, just at that hour in a late summer day when the sun is already below the horizon and the risen full moon in the visible sky stops being chalky and begins to take on light. There comes the moment, and I saw it then, when the moon goes from flat to round. For the first time it met my eyes as a globe. The word 'moon' came into my mouth as though fed to me out of a silver spoon. Held in my mouth it became a word." Welty used her observations about the details of nature as ingredients for her ideas. Blended together they become the powerful messages of her writing.

Observers love to watch. They are fascinated by human behavior. They can stand for hours in awe of nature and regularly see something new. You recognize these folks because they like to crowd watch, nature walk, or just plain observe. From the outside looking in, they may seem stagnant, but their curiosity is fully throttled.

My four-year-old daughter came home from preschool and I asked her what she had done that day. She replied, "I looked and looked." Of course, she is a genius in training, but the point is, Observers feel comfortable looking around, scanning their environment for what interests them. Even when standing outside the activity, they wonder why things are the way they are. When you were a child, I'm sure you used this skill on a regular basis. But as we get older and busier, our sense of observation wains. We catch only the things that scan as "critical" and we lose the ingredients that make great Observer insights. We miss the small details—the new words of a teenager, the tone of a colleague's voice, the unusual shifts in your industry that are the grist for new ideas. We stop watching and start plodding.

Consider the consumate watcher Leonardo da Vinci, the great painter, inventor, and architect. Da Vinci threw parties for peasants in his town. He didn't do this because he was kindhearted or generous, but because he wanted to watch the peasants—study their faces, their movements, and how they interacted with one another. His observations were the basis for his drawings of the human face and his study of anatomy. His genius was the ability to stand in awe, notice things that piqued his interest, and make profound conclusions about their meaning. What others easily passed over, he cherished as the pathway to breakthrough.

Observers have the ability to stand in awe and wait for an inspiration. They know when to "go slow." As you learn to selectively slow your mental pace, you can capture some of the genius of the Observer.

OBSERVERS CHERISH THE DETAIL OTHERS FIND ORDINARY

Collecting and analyzing the detail, like a sleuth, is the means to a creative end for the Observer. You and I may become frustrated by the small things, but they are the Observer's center of discovery. So while they watch, they are in a constant search for some small thing worthy of their attention.

The seventeenth-century Dutch painter Jan Vermeer forever changed the discipline of European painting by being one of the first artists to master detail in his work. He was captivated by the small things and manipulated them to perfection. Vermeer painted one particular composition again and again—light streaming through a window illuminating a single person in contemplation. He paid close attention to how the light reflected in the room, how it turned iridescent on a brass pitcher, and how it made fabric transparent. It is said his genius was his "passion for observation." Vermeer used detail to tell the exceptional story of mundane moments when an individual is alone with his thoughts.

My undergraduate degree was in art, and a required course was still-life drawing. One of the class exercises was to draw a large plant placed at the front of the room. I spent my time laboring over the proportions of the plant. Were the leaves tall enough in relation to the pot? Where did the leaves attach to the stem? I spent the session mastering my eraser. I glanced at my neighbor's work. I was stunned. She spent the hour concentrating on only the roots of the plant. Her composition focused on the complicated tangle of the many plant stems, how they twisted and wrapped around each other. The drawing was incredibly beautiful and used detail to tell a story about the plant that I had missed.

Think about the music legend Bob Dylan. He used the skills of the Observer to write some of the most potent songs of the last century—"Like a Rolling Stone" or "Blowin' in the Wind." His greatest lyrics were born from paying attention to the simplest details of his experience and then expressing them in a creative way. His biographer said: "The key to Bob's genius lay in his ability to spin folk-style songs from observation. Bob seized little moments from his life, exaggerated them to fit a particular theme, and came up with a new, entertaining song." Seizing little moments, fitting them to a theme, and coming up with something new—these are tools Observers use to move from status quo to breakthrough.

Also captivated by observations, the anthropologist Margaret Mead studied adolescents growing up in Samoa. She spent hours watching their everyday lives and keeping detailed journals about their rituals and customs. While she observed simple behaviors that others took for granted, she made creative conclusions about adolescence that proved to be enlightening to the study of human character and social structures. It was said of her, "Wherever she went in her nearly seventy-seven years, she called attention to the ordinary, the previously unsung, and she sanctified the mundane."

At first some people find it difficult to slow down enough to notice the small things, but it is really easier than you may think. Once you begin to see the value in the details, you'll start to find wonderful capabilities within. Your creative spirit just needs a little ammunition.

CURIOSITY IS THE HALLMARK OF THE OBSERVER

All of the Five Faces of Genius are driven by a spirit of curiosity. As the advertising great Leo Burnett said, "Curiosity is the secret of great creative people." The Observer's curiosity is relentless. Her creative fire feeds on it like oxygen. Curiosity propels Observers to find themes between the details, which become catalysts for big ideas. You can frequently identify an Observer by his constant reference to the question "Why?"

Thomas Edison, whose inventions ranged from the incandescent light to the phonograph, was called an "inquisitive question-box." As a young boy "he ran down to the shipyards and watched the men building boats for Great Lakes shipping. There he asked the shipbuilders hundreds of questions. Why could you see a hammer hit a board before you could hear it, if you were at a distance? Why did you have to fit joints carefully? What was pitch made of?" If others were unable to answer his questions, he would ask, "Why *don't* you know?" Edison was hounded by the "Why" question of curiosity.

Leonardo da Vinci was also a relentless question asker. He was called "the arbiter of all questions." The cultural critic Kenneth Clark describes him as "the most relentlessly curious man in history. Everything he saw made him ask why and how. . . . Reading the thousands of words in Leonardo's note-books, one is absolutely worn out by this energy. He won't take yes for an answer. He can't leave anything alone—he worries it, re-states it, answers imaginary antagonists."

Listen to how Richard Feynman described the terrain of his curiosity: "In my room at Princeton I had a bay window with a U-shaped window-sill. One day some ants came out on the windowsill and wandered around a little bit. I got curious as to how they found things. I wondered, how do they know where to go? Can they tell each other where food is, like bees can? Do they have any sense of geometry?" He went on to talk about the ad hoc experiments he set up to answer his own questions. Each question was a well he needed to pump until it was dry.

The Observer takes poet Rainer Maria Rilke's admonition seriously: "Try to love the questions themselves." When you follow your curiosity, you'll discover what truly interests you, and you may even begin to discover the link between your responsibilities and your passions.

OBSERVERS ARE COMPELLED BY BEAUTY

They are awestruck by it. For them, beauty is the gateway to truth. They are willing to wait, to breathe, to anticipate the experience of nature, and to find inspiration. George Eliot said she was going to write a novel inspired by "the breath of cows and the scent of hay." The poet Walt Whitman waited in nature: "I loaf and invite my soul." Beauty invites inspiration.

In order to wait for beauty, Observers follow Plato's suggestion and let themselves be quiet. "If we could be quiet we could hear the symphony of the spheres." Nature invites the purest of inspiration. Beauty feeds the creative soul.

When you begin to explore your Observer skills, you'll find yourself digging up beauty in the oddest places. You'll notice special moments when people work especially well together and you'll wonder why. You'll find work environments that seem aesthetically pleasing and wonder how you can replicate them. You'll find competitors that are doing things with an aura of beauty and wonder how you can challenge them. Beauty will become a beacon to guide your creative spirit.

Now it may seem strange to talk about slowing down and standing in awe of beauty in a book about business, but the truth is, those who find creative breakthroughs at work are tuned in to these ethereal concepts. Let's explore how.

Mastering the Observer at Work

Before Howard Schultz became the CEO of Starbucks, he was a salesman for a housewares company called Hammarplast, which sold a cone-shaped coffee filter with an attached Thermos. Popular for brewing coffee in Europe, these filters had yet to catch on in the United States. However, Schultz noticed a curious detail. One small retailer in Seattle was selling an inordinate number of these items. Why would one customer require so many cones and thermoses? He pursued his question and flew to Seattle to investigate Starbucks, then a small coffee retailer selling a lot of brewing paraphernalia. Enchanted with the concept of fresh-roasted, high-quality coffee, Schultz bought the fledgling bean retailer and eventually introduced the concept of gourmet coffee bars across America and around the world.

Paying attention to details and drawing creative conclusions from them is a vital skill in today's business renaissance. When you master this Face, you'll uncover a gold mine. Let's dig down and see how business geniuses have used their Observer skills to move from status quo to breakthrough. As you explore the Observer, you'll learn to make big ideas at work.

GET YOUR CURIOSITY OUT OF JAIL

Walt Disney started his career as an illustrator. He loved to draw cartoons and characters, yet his colleagues were interested in animation. He was curious about how animation worked. He spent his outside time learning from his friends how movies were made. Disney said, "I might have become a political cartoonist, except that I was exposed to movie cartoons at the Kansas City Film Ad Company. There were a lot of cartoonists there, but none of them had my ambition to do anything else. The artist just did his work and turned it over to the cameraman to photograph. But I wasn't satisfied with that. I watched the cameraman do his work, and I asked questions, "What's your exposure?" "Why do you shoot it that way?" He was secretive at first but then told me all about it, and he let me run the camera myself. So I learned . . ." It was Disney's curiosity that led to mastering animated film production and was his start in breakthrough movies.

When practicing your Observer skills, imagine you are walking around with a cartoon bubble over your head that says, "What does this mean? What can I learn from it?" The questions go with you wherever you go. Be sure to let that curiosity travel with you. Don't let circumstances snuff it out. Remember, it's only when we pursue our questions that our creative spirit can thrive.

Lani is a territory manager for a company that sells foam insulation. Her customer wanted to ship lamp shades across the world, and it was imperative that they arrive in perfect condition. Lani suggested packaging and shipping ten lamp shades from ten different locations all over the globe to the company headquarters to see if the material would be suitable for the job. When the lamp shades returned, they were all in perfect condition. They were not bent or injured, and even when the box was damaged, the lamp shades looked great. However, one detail bothered Lani. When she opened the box shipped from Mexico, there was an unpleasant fume, a chemical scent. "It was as if I couldn't turn off my curiosity. I had to get to the bottom of this weird smell."

At home that night, Lani noticed on the news that there was a record heat wave in Mexico. She took the insulation material to the engineering department, and when they tested the insulation in extreme heat and humidity, it began to fume. Her test revealed a problem that could have been disastrous for this client. "My curiosity led me to discover a problem and I was able to set the creative process in motion and design a custom product for extreme temperatures." Her curiosity led to insight.

Observers often say, "I'm curious about . . ." I describe Observers as the children's book character Curious George. Curious George is a monkey who gets in trouble because he is so curious. He investigates everything that piques his interest. If Observers get into trouble it's because everything interests them. For instance, Observers get in trouble in book stores. They are so curious about everything they can't decide where to concentrate.

Cooking? Literature? Biography? Technology? They may even buy too many books. Yet it's the Observers' insatiable curiosity that leads them to breakthroughs.

Try these excercises to get your curiosity out of jail:

1. Become a Curious George.

Exercise your natural curiosity. Begin to wonder why. The next time you are confronted with something that seems different or "off," ask yourself, "What are the reasons this is happening in my work? Why now?"

2. Observe your customers.

Watch your customers interact with the product even though you've seen it before. Listen to your clients' new research even though you've already heard similar information. You may be able to unearth something no one else has thought about.

CONNECT THE DETAIL DOTS

Once Observers collect their information, they begin a process I call "connecting the detail dots." They find a way to bring all the important details together to create a business insight. In fact, Schultz's Starbucks inspiration is filled with Observer details. He noticed an espresso bar while on a walk in Milan. Sometime later he noticed another and another. He writes, "My mind started churning." It was during these walks in Italy that he realized Starbucks should move from selling beans alone to serving fresh coffee, and the concept was born. He realized, "Serving espresso drinks the Italian way could be the differentiating factor for Starbucks." Schultz demonstrates the sensitivity of the painter Vermeer, watching the details, paying attention to the environment around him, and connecting the dots for an idea. When you learn to stand in awe of what is happening before you and connect the details, you'll find the magical moments of inspiration Schultz found. Our business genius is just below the surface when we make big ideas from small ingredients.

Notice how similar Schultz's story is to the ingenuity of Ray Kroc and his breakthrough called McDonald's? They both noticed what others might perceive as detail—one small customer's sales history. Their Observer curiosity was piqued. Each noticed data, connected the dots, and exploited the idea before anyone else did. When you become alert to the small things, genius ideas are born.

Now some folks say, "I'm not interested in small things. I'm paid to look at the big picture. It's the macroperspective that interests me." But remember, Observers are not interested in detail for its own sake. They are only interested in details as ingredients of a new idea. Your key to the Observer skill is knowing when and where to use it. The smart Observer knows what data to collect and when to turn off the radar. The goal is to be able to float between looking for details and appreciating the macroperspective.

Try these exercises now:

1. Learn to selectively slow down.

Choose times you will intentionally work slowly and notice small things. Choose a specific area of your work—say, while you are in staff meetings, or during a customer visit, or while you write a weekly report. Choose a time that has potential for inspiration. Selectively slowing down means keeping your antennae tuned to creative detail that may be surfacing. During this interval, let yourself notice little clues. You will discover a whole basket of stimuli that could become a creative new idea.

2. Practice hypothesizing.

Choose a current situation at work and ask yourself what could the details mean? What larger issues do these details reflect? Give yourself lots of options. Create three or four ideas about what the details mean. Use these hypotheses as the foundation of your ideas. Try to connect the dots.

Our creative strength depends on occasionally dipping into the water of details. A market with a small sales decrease. An overheard conversation. An offhand competitor comment. After a while we become seasoned. We become business artists. We realize which details are worthy of our consideration and which are a waste of our time. We begin to walk the line of wisdom. You can learn to move back and forth between ignoring details and worshipping them as the ingredients of ideas.

OBSERVERS PAY ATTENTION TO WHISPERS

Observers are especially good at spotting business trends before they take off and fly. Steve Jobs says, "I've always paid attention to the whispers around me." By listening to the whispers, you can be the business artist who identifies opportunity first.

Pierre Omidyar originated the electronic commerce site called eBay. His inspiration came when his girlfriend, who collected Pez candy dispensers, offhandedly complained that it was hard to find them. For Omidyar this was a "whisper." His ears went up. He wondered how many others had a hard time finding sellers and buyers of collectibles. He created the online auction service by noticing a whisper—a comment by his girlfriend—which represented a big opportunity. eBay now has a net worth of $906.4 million.

Some firms put those with Observer skills in the market to notice trends before a wave begins to swell. Levi Strauss, makers of the American icon Levi's, puts designers into the market to build personal relationships with consumers. If the designers know their customers' interests—where they shop, where they party, what they like—the designers are more likely to create the next best jean. They'll hear the whispers—the colors that are hip, the way people wear their pants, what they need to carry in their pockets. Levi's wants business artists who will notice the small things, the details, and develop a new fad. When your Observer skills grow, you learn to accurately predict with only a few clues.

Dominant Observers would often rather watch and wonder than be obviously engaged. They are listening for whispers with which to analyze people and situations. Akio Morita, founder of Sony, used his Observer skills to create one of the greatest products of the twentieth century, the Sony Walkman. Morita was fascinated by why people listened to music and how they interacted with the stereo. He watched his children lug equipment to the beach to enjoy music. With the same intense observation of Leonardo da Vinci's peasant watching, Morita sought to understand the hidden reasons behind listening to music.

While observing, Morita had an insight. Why should you have to haul equipment around to take music with you? What if you could easily bring music everywhere you went? This inspiration was the birth of the Sony Walkman, the revolutionary product that made music truly portable.

T. S. Eliot said the job of the poet was to raid the inarticulate. When you are a business artist, you raid the inarticulated needs of the customer. What do your customers want? What haven't they yet articulated? The Observer listens for the whisper and finds the idea.

Think of the big retailers, the one-stop shopping stores like Wal-Mart, Kmart, or Costco. Until the advent of these alternatives, we didn't know we needed them. We were content to go to the local hardware store, or buy our toys at the drugstore. Now it's hard to believe we could live without these megacenters. But would anyone have said, "I'd really like one large store where I could get all my home, hardware needs, and groceries met in one trip"? These companies were poets and discovered the unarticulated needs.

Have you listened for the whispers of how hard it is to be a customer of your company? Or how hard it is to be a colleague working with your team? Have you paid attention to the details and appreciated what it's like to work with you?

"Sometimes it's hard to be a customer of this firm. I really wanted to change that." Tim is a salesperson for a manufacturing company. Tim's dominant creative style is that of an Observer. He had billed a customer several invoices and it had been more than sixty days and his firm had received no payment. Tim's accounting department had been bugging him to call his clients to get paid.

When he got through to the clients and asked why the bills had taken so long, Tim found differing responses. One bill sat on someone's desk. Another client thought the bill was an estimate, not an invoice. Someone else didn't notice the due date. Yet another required all invoicing via e-mail.

Instead of blaming his clients for their ineptitude, Tim thought these signs may be whispers of what his clients really needed from him. Perhaps his firm's invoicing process should be redesigned. He spearheaded an electronic billing process for all his firm's clients that saved the firm money and made clients happy. Tim said, "I worked with accounting to redesign the graphics on bills as well as the e-mail delivery. I realized that creative insight happens when you listen to what your clients need that they don't even ask for."

If you want to improve your Observer skills and hear the whispers of unarticulated needs, try these exercises:

1. Notice things that are discomforting in your work.

What bothers you? What do you think bothers your customers? What are the problems you have with clients?

List your discomforts on paper—the frustrating phone call with a colleague; the irritated customer; the meeting with your boss that went poorly. Use your curiosity. Why are these things the way they are? See what solutions you can generate. Problems have a way of snapping our minds to attention. They will lead you to new solutions and imaginative ideas.

2. Ask yourself the question "What is my customer looking for and can't find?"

Don't just think of what you currently offer. Dream with a wide perspective. What *could* you offer?

Don't forget to think of your colleagues and co-workers as customers. What do they need that is not yet articulated? Providing fresh solutions is how idea leaders are born.

APPRECIATE BEAUTY IN YOUR WORK

Let me show you how the Observer's obsession with beauty translates to business.

Kim is a meeting planner who puts together conference events for a telecommunications firm. After setting up a meeting and waiting for guests to arrive, she checks the "feel" of the environment. At one particularly important meeting, she did just that and noticed small things that could be improved. She had the air-conditioning turned off—it was too loud and distracting and instead had the windows in the meeting room opened to provide fresh air. She had cut lemons put in the water pitchers. She asked for additional porch space so participants could get better cell phone reception during the meeting breaks. Kim says, "I try to add some small special touches to everything I do. It's like I'm an artist, and I put my creative signature on my work." It's the power of beauty, the small things that define our creativity in the business renaissance.

Think of your best customer service experience. It was an encounter of care and kindness: the phone operator who was kind and helped you get what you need, the flight attendant who tried to make you more comfortable when it seemed impossible, the sales rep who genuinely cared and made your job easier, the co-worker who goes to bat for you. When you promote beauty, you can discover genius ideas.

Consider the manager who wonders why business is going so well at her office supply store. She asks customers questions about products they like. She asks them why they shop here instead of elsewhere. What store hours best suit them? She is constantly tinkering with her service to make sure her store is the preferred choice in the market. She wants the experience to be one of beauty.

If you want to bring wonder to your work, begin to appreciate beautiful things. Become a student of beauty. Pay attention to the clouds in the sky, the way snowflakes cluster, the quality of light in different rooms. Try to see beauty in mundane things. Practicing the presence of beauty strengthens your ability to observe the details of life. This will have spill-over effects into your work.

Business artists find passion and meaning at work. They see beauty and work as a continuum.

The Observer can help you launch your genius. Slow down and promote beauty:

1. Make a list of what you do well in your work.

What is elegant and beautiful about what you do every day? Do you listen well? Do you make others' lives easier? Search for the small things.

2. Mentally stand in awe of your customers.

What do they do well? How do they manage many pressures and still succeed? If you could assist them further, what opportunities do you notice?

Here is a summary of the key business principles of the Observer:

1. Get your curiosity out of jail: Relentlessly wonder why.
2. Pay attention to whispers: Listen for peripheral ideas that could indicate trends.

3. Connect the detail dots: Watch for small influences and look for themes.

4. Appreciate beauty in your work: Strive for aesthetics, care, and kindness in your business.

Observers and Teams

Observers are the "creative conscience" of the group. Their ideas have integrity because they are firmly rooted in the real problems of the business—real information, real customers, real concerns. They hypothesize potential solutions based on the issues. Observers succeed in business because they are sensitive observers of the work around them *and* make unique contributions. You'll find Observers concentrated in research, engineering, strategy and planning, analysis, and operations functions.

The Observers' curiosity propels teams to new ideas. Their curiosity drives the group forward; their questions often lead the group process. Their conceptual thinking skills become guides. Observers have insightful and important ideas to share and groups find their ongoing contributions very valuable.

There is a high correlation between Observers and introversion. Much of Observers' creative process happens while they are alone. They can fill their imagination on their own so the team experience of creativity may seem less valuable to them. Because innovation is a conceptual process, they will often come to the group with a myriad of solutions they have already developed on their own. Teams need Observers more than Observers perceive they need the team.

So be patient with Observers. Because information is their primary stimulus, Observers often need data to begin their ideation process. They will become easily frustrated by a group brainstorming with no real stimulus to begin.

For example, if you are working on a creative solution for a software redesign, the Observer may stop the process midstream and say, "We need to sit with some customers for a while and determine what the real issues are." While this may be needed, it tends to aggravate other team members who are ready to create. A Seer might be ready to share two or three pictures they've created in their mind's eye. A Sage might have an insight to share. But the Observer may feel the group hasn't yet defined the problem.

Because you'll want to ensure Observers are happy team members, honor their creative style. You may have to adapt the group process to ensure you've given the Observer enough information. Provide the data or details that you will be discussing in advance. An Observer will most likely have more to contribute if you give him time to review the information before the team meets. Do everything you can to maximize the group experience for the Observer. You'll see immediate rewards.

AN OBSERVER TEAM EXERCISE

Try an exercise called "Coalescing." Ask team members to bring information they've noticed around a business issue for discussion. Let's say you're meeting to decide how to deliver customer orders more quickly. One member might bring in a customer letter complaining about their service. Another person might bring in a story about how another firm solved a similar problem. Another person might bring in a flow chart of the current process as they see it. Ask each participant to explain what they've brought and why, and post it around the conference room. Together the team works to coalesce—find unusual and unique themes. You'll find you can discover new ways of looking at the information and create solutions together.

Observer Pitfalls to Avoid

There are a few areas that can trip up Observers and limit their ability to be idea champions. First, be sure to have a good cross-section of detail in your data pool. For example, you may be a human resources manager and believe the company hires people who are too similar to one another, but you may have looked at only one department, or at one level of employees. Be sure you've collected the right data. Are you observing the right details?

The second stumbling block is forgetting to make the conceptual contribution after analyzing the detail. We all know detail-oriented people. They are great at telling you what is wrong, but they forget to make any creative hypothesis from the detail. *The Observer's creative skill is in this dual action of noticing the detail and then making a creative contribution from it.* Don't forget to make the leaps and the ingenious hypotheses.

The Observer brings you closer to your creative genius. By selectively slowing down, you encounter the mystery that brings meaning to work. Honor your curiosity and your questions. These are the gateways to the creative life of the business artist.

The Five Faces of Genius Summary

	THE SEER	THE OBSERVER	THE ALCHEMIST	THE FOOL	THE SAGE
The Creative Power Principle	The Power to Image	The Power to Notice Detail	The Power to Connect Domains	The Power to Celebrate Weakness	The Power to Simplify
Key Creative Skill	Visualization	Ideas from the collection of detail Curiosity			
Easy Way to Remember the Face	See it	Notice it			
Benefit to Teams	Vision for future Test possible outcomes	Conceptual thinking rooted in real issues			
Pitfalls	Needs to combine Seer with other Faces	Needs to collect a variety of details			

Exercises

When change comes crashing in, those who notice it first capitalize on it and claim the opportunity. You can learn from the Observer how to notice the small things around you and sense the waves of change first. Begin by working on the following exercises to strengthen your Observer side.

1. Think back over your business responsibilites in the last few months. What have you noticed lately that has made you curious? What have you wondered about? What has surprised you? Any mysteries? Pay attention to the small things, details you may not have noticed before. List four things you now notice in review.

1)

2)

3)

4)

Define the central challenge that you face at work today.

Write it here: _____

Now, use the "Five Why's" discipline: Ask yourself five times for the reason why this is happening. Answer the question "Why is this happening?" and then repeat the question four more times and answer it in the spaces below. What ideas surface?

1)

2)

3)

4)

5)

How the Observer Creates Innovation Rituals

The Observer knows how to slow down and watch and wait for ideas. One of the ways this slowing down happens is through the use of rituals. Rituals are the practice of doing something over and over again and waiting for ideas to strike.

You've heard the slam, "The definition of insanity is doing the same thing over and over again and expecting different results." Well, Observers do the same things again and again and get different results. They use ritual as a means to innovation. Here are some rituals leading innovators use to protect their business inspiration.

1. Make commuting time sacred.

If you ask business artists when they get their best work ideas, they answer while they drive, or take the train or bus to work. They use commuting time to solve problems, review issues in their mind, or tackle new challenges. With the advent of voice mail, the time that was once devoted to inspiration has turned into an administration opium. Now we answer voice mail on our cell phones. Find another time to do voice mail. Reserve this sacred commuting time for ideas.

2. Make air travel sacred.

Another place business artists get ideas is while traveling on an airplane. When locked in a plane, we can do little but decompress and just think. With the advent of e-mail download, the time that was once devoted to contemplation has also turned into an administration opium. We now try to answer our e-mail while we fly. Find another time to do e-mail. Make idea time during travel a ritual.

3. Don't manage your work; manage your meetings.

Meetings are the single biggest time wasters of managers trying to become business artists. You can easily get to the point where your calendar is running you.

Substitute innovation time for noncritical meetings, teams, and assignments. Set high standards for meetings you will attend. Get it out of the others. Remember: It's an idea economy, not an administrative one!

Spend your saved time thinking, dreaming, innovating.

4. Use meeting downtime as mind time.

Only about 25 percent of meeting content requires your focused attention. Master mentally checking in and out of meetings. Use the other 75 percent of the time to dream about the challenges you face. Learn to use a business journal (see page 88) and take notes about your questions and challenges during meetings. Refine your ability to move easily between group contribution and personal mind time.

5. Don't wait to innovate.

I used to try to get all my administrative tasks done and my desk cleared before I started tackling a business problem that needed a creative solution. We mistakenly think that if our desk is clean, there will be space for ideas to land. But I can tell you that it's impossible to innovate that way. Your voice mail light will always flash. Your e-mail will always announce that you have mail. There will always be someone asking for your help.

Live like the artist. Artists easily toggle back and forth between art and administration. Use small chunks of available time for focusing your creative spirit.

6. Find a safe haven for inspiration.

I had a client whose building was next to a Dunkin' Donuts. I would make a practice of arriving at Dunkin' Donuts about one hour before my meeting would start. I'd plan, think about the future, think about the next surprise I could create for the client. I'd get ideas. Dunkin' Donuts was a holy place. Plus, I really loved the apple fritters.

Find a mundane place where you can dream—a walking trail, a fast-food restaurant, a vista. Find a place that inspires you and think about the business mysteries there.

7. Make your own innovation ritual.

3M developed a 15 percent rule. Fifteen percent of researchers' time can be spent on projects of their own interest. Researchers are free to investigate opportunities and don't even need to discuss the subject of their exploration with their supervisors. The intention of the ritual is to give researchers the energy they need to pursue new ideas.

Allocate some time every week for innovation. Carve out a couple of hours a week or even a morning a week for dreaming about the possibilities of the business. Use the time to take a supplier to lunch to talk about new ideas. Read what's new in other industries and other companies. Take time to surf the Web to see what's hot. Make it ritual.

Ideas Through Technology Deprivation

"It's what Goethe said in Faust—that technology is not going to save us. Our computers, our tools, our machines are not enough. We have to rely on our intuition, our true being."
—JOSEPH CAMPBELL

Observers know there's no debate that business technology has revolutionized work in positive ways. But as much as technology has helped us, it also damages our business creativity. The Observer teaches us to slow down, to wait, to look at the peripheral, to consider the fringes. In order for imagination to lead implementation, we need to deprive ourselves of technology.

Here's what I mean. Computer logic is tight, flawless. It's based on the notion of if/then thinking. If x is true, then y is or is not true. Conclusions from technological tools are linear. They have no messy margins. Computer logic misses the tangential idea. It doesn't allow for spin-off thinking and even *il*logic that often leads to breakthrough ideas. While writing this book, I needed a thesaurus. My word-processing program had a thesaurus function in the software. So I used it, but I hungered for something more.

I found an old *Roget's Thesaurus* and started thumbing through. By simply flipping through the pages I stumbled upon great words from random sections. I made unconscious connections. I would have never found these words by using the software.

William Blake said, "Improvements make straight roads but the crooked roads without improvement are the roads of genius." Technology doesn't promote the crooked roads.

Think of a time you've seen computer analysis presented. We see current numbers, future estimates, and even long-range forecasts. The sheer scope of the information dupes us into believing the conclusions from the computer are gospel. It's tight. It looks good. Funny thing though, when you dig deeper you find messy margins. The numbers were wrong. The model made assumptions based on the wrong parameters. The forecasts were overblown. It looks pretty but the conclusions can be flawed. Technology can focus us on the *presentation* of the information instead of the *ideas* about the information.

Here are some way to preserve our inspiration for ideas:

1. Wean yourself away from e-mail.

Since the inception of e-mail, we spend an average of thirty minutes every day answering messages in front of the computer. This is thirty incremental minutes of administration we didn't previously have. In most firms the demand for paper has gone up 30 percent. More people are sending more communication to one another and we are *printing it out!* So much for the paperless society. The antidote to this maelstrom of overcommunication is to refuse to play the game.

Limit e-mail to low-priority communication, wide-scale communication, or chatting. Business artists know nothing critical gets communicated by e-mail. It's too easy to share, too easy to screw up, and too easy to miscommunicate. Many of us have an e-mail horror story where something valuable was mistakenly sent to the wrong person. Or something was interpreted the wrong way. So, cherry-pick which e-mails you will send and read and delete the rest.

2. Use your head, not your keyboard.

When you need to communicate something important, start with a blank piece of paper and put your central message in a circle in the middle of the page. Then write the key thoughts around the circle. How do you want to introduce the idea? What are your support statements? What will your conclusion be? Draw some wild thoughts. Sketch out a chart.

Once you've drawn the communication in long hand, then word process. Managers sit in front of the computer writing/rewriting because we don't yet know what we want to say. We waste more time trying to jam our thoughts into the parameters of the software than it would take to word process what we compose by hand. Don't let the computer dominate your creative process.

3. Selectively ignore voice mail.

Many business artists find it helpful to listen to voice mail only once or twice during the day. Now you may be thinking, "I could never do that." I'd miss deadlines, projects. Yet thought leaders report they typically check it only twice, before work and at the close of the day. Avoiding voice mail slows down your pace and gives you time to use your brain during the day to think. Instead of putting out fires, you have time to start your own.

4. Resurrect old business traditions.

Steven Spielberg uses an old-fashioned machine to edit his films. He purposely avoids the newer technology because the old style is slower and gives him regular breaks. He says he needs the frequent seven- to eight-minute breaks the old machine provides because he has time to reflect on the creative work he is doing.

Some of the old traditions give us time to reflect on what we are doing. How about business lunches? How about wine with lunch? How about face-to-face meetings with colleagues instead of video conferencing? How about the art of a memo?

The Observer cherishes the messy margins, the art of the peripheral. The Observer knows the technology will not save us—or our business. Our salvation is our own intuition.

3. THE ALCHEMIST

THE POWER TO CONNECT DOMAINS

"I wish to live as to derive my inspiration from the commonest events,
so that what my senses may perceive, my daily walk,
the conversation with my neighbors, may inspire me and I
may dream of no heaven but that which lies about me."

—HENRY DAVID THOREAU

When you ask Arthur Martinez, CEO of Sears, Roebuck and Company, for his vision of the future, he says he wants a brand with the power of Disney. Steve Case, CEO of America Online, creates ideas for Internet content by looking to television networks like NBC. Alchemists get their ideas, as Thoreau said, from that which lies about them. They make connections between their world and the worlds of others, and in the association come up with great breakthroughs.

Alchemy is the ancient art of mixing base metals with hopes of creating gold. Alchemists combined natural elements to create medicines and healing potions. They would mix chemicals and try to develop magical results. Today's Alchemists might connect plant biology to human development or connect themes from physics to music. Or like a colleague of mine, business to golf, football, basketball, baseball. You get the story. Alchemists steal ideas from one area and apply them to another. This leads to great insights in art, science, and business genius.

The third Face of Genius is the Alchemist, or the principle of connection. The Alchemist brings together two separate domains—different interests, disciplines, or systems of thought, and connects them in a unique way to develop a breakthrough. The three prongs of mastery are:

1. Alchemists borrow ideas.
2. Alchemists' broad range of interests drive their ideas.
3. Alchemists find insight in connections.

The Creative Genius of the Alchemist: Spark Connections to Create Electric Ideas

Frank Lloyd Wright was a seminal architect whose body of work spanned seven decades, and he created some of the most original buildings in the history of American architecture. His style was a melding, an alchemy, of the architectural design and the organic world surrounding it. He broke down the boundaries between inside and outside spaces by filling large walls with spans of windows. He designed buildings over waterfalls. Instead of cutting down trees, he built a house around them. He designed a table with a hole in the center so that something from nature—a twig, a rock, a plant—could regularly be brought inside and placed there. Even in something as small as a table, Wright illustrates his Alchemist spirit by mixing the domain of nature with the domain of the building.

You can discover unique ideas—electric ideas—by bringing unexpected things together. You can make connections and sense the similarities between what you see around you and what you do at work. Learn from the Alchemist. Look for connections.

ALCHEMISTS' INSIGHTS COME FROM BORROWING IDEAS

Alchemists are not shy about what others might think of as "copying." Consider Michelangelo's painting of the Sistine Chapel. This labor took him many years and through it all he struggled in body and soul because he never wanted to paint it in the first place. Even though he was a talented painter, Michelangelo thought of himself as a sculptor. He didn't have the same passion for painting as for sculpting. But Pope Julius II was insistent that Michelangelo work his genius on the chapel. Frustrated, Michelangelo kept the chapel locked and let no one watch him while he worked.

Raphael, a contemporary of Michelangelo and an accomplished painter himself, got to thinking: "What was Michelangelo's idea for the painting? What did the ceiling look like? What new techniques had he developed?" Raphael couldn't stand it. He had the key to the chapel stolen. One night, Raphael unlocked the door, crept in, and surreptitiously gazed at the masterpiece in progress. Raphael was overwhelmed.

One of Raphael's most famous works is called *The School of Athens*. In this portrait, Raphael depicts many people of the Greek court. The figures are delicately portrayed in Raphael's characteristic smooth and elegant style—all the figures except one. In the foreground is a powerful man displayed in very different form with heavy features and sculpted musculature. This figure is Raphael's self-portrait. Art critics agree Raphael copied Michelangelo's style from the stolen glance at the ceiling of the Sistine Chapel. Raphael copied Michelangelo yet created an original expression.

Now this doesn't mean you want to blantantly go around taking the ideas of others and claiming them as your own. But bringing elements of others' work to your own is a natural part of the creative process. Alchemists are always searching for the similarities that will provide the spark of invention.

Sir Issac Newton said, "I stand on the shoulders of giants." Newton knew that invention is sometimes assembled by borrowing pieces of ideas from others. Picasso said, "Copy others, just don't copy yourself." Invention can be cut from the cloth of someone else's labor.

The contemporary movie *Rushmore* was directed by Wes Anderson. Anderson admits some of his inspiration came from the movie *The Graduate*. Anderson says he stole the scene from *The Graduate* in which Dustin Hoffman dives into the swimming pool and hesitates at the bottom of the pool, pondering his fate. In *Rushmore*, Bill Murray does the same thing—dives into the pool and meditates at the bottom about his dislike for his twin sons.

Do you live under the leaky roof that original ideas have to be wholly your own? Alchemists borrow ideas wherever they can find them and use them to make their unique breakthroughs. Leaning on others can be a pathway to building innovations. In the land of ideas, no one is an island.

When you've welcomed the Alchemist into your creative style, you'll find yourself scanning your environment for ideas you can borrow. Whatever your challenges, you'll trust there will be solutions lying all around.

ALCHEMISTS' BROAD RANGE OF INTERESTS DRIVE INVENTION

Alchemists use their interests in many fields to make creative connections. Leonardo da Vinci brought mathematics to his painting. He was one of the first artists to apply the scientific calculations of perspective to his work. The mathematical composition that underlies *The Last Supper* is one of the attributes that makes it so memorable. James Michener brought his love of history to novels. Mary Cassatt connected her interests in the relationship between mothers and children to her painting. It is this broad range of interests that makes creative genius so fertile.

When you talk with Alchemists, it's difficult to find a subject that *doesn't* interest them. They love to play in a big field and find lots of ideas. One Alchemist told me, "I can find something interesting in just about anything I read—even an airline magazine!"

Do you have a friend like this? I do. Tina knows lots of things about many areas. I'm always amazed at the wealth of information living in her head. She doesn't care about being a subject-matter expert in any one area. She's sampler of many. She can tell you about dog breeding. She knows about DNA typing. She can survey trends in the health-care industry. She reads something and it sticks with her. She uses all her interests as a springboard to new ideas.

Because Alchemists create ideas through connections, new environments become critically important. They need to be working in situations in which their interests can be sparked. They need to be exposed to the people, the ideas, the physical world that will provide the connections they need. Listen to the Alchemist at work in the mind of Bob Dylan. "Bob had an ear that was finely tuned to conversation. He would eavesdrop on people and scribble down things they said. Or he'd lift ideas from rap sessions with his friends. . . . Somebody would read or tell him something about a poet or an artist, he'd use it to produce something uniquely his own . . . Then later I'd hear what they said in a slightly different way from in one of his songs. He was influenced by everything and everybody." Alchemists put themselves in places where their spirits will be nourished.

Conversation is essential to the creative process of the Alchemist. The ideas of others often form the springboard from which genius ideas are born. T. S. Eliot's most famous poem is "The Waste Land." When Eliot first wrote the piece it was more than one thousand lines and he was not happy with it. He felt too close to the poem to critique it. So Eliot passed it on to his two closest friends—his wife and Ezra Pound, another poet. Both believed the poem was too long and began editing. By the time Eliot's poem was published, it only had five hundred lines. Contemporary literary critics agree that had Eliot submitted the poem at one thousand lines, it would never have received popular acclaim. Alchemists rely with great trust upon the connections made between the ideas of others and their own.

If you want to grow your Alchemist side, it's important to keep a wide range of conversations going. Talk to different people about different ideas. Keep meetings open-ended to let free discussions and tangential ideas flow. The Alchemist needs the spark that dialogue provides.

THE ALCHEMIST FINDS INSIGHTS IN CONNECTIONS

Most of us put work in a box, far away from the rest of our life. But the Alchemist knows ideas come from work, from play, from rest, from just about anywhere—as Thoreau said, from the "commonest events." Alchemists are always listening for the muse's voice. The creative life is one swath of fabric that cannot be torn into a piece called work and a piece called play.

Clients who are Alchemists often comment they can't "turn work off." But this isn't a negative for them. Because their creativity is alive at work, ideas for work percolate after hours. Their life flows as one natural continuum and they find creative expression in all they do.

The philosopher Krishnamurti said in 1934, "To me, the true artist is one who lives completely, harmoniously, who does not divide his art from living, whose very life is that expression . . . who has not divorced his expression on a canvas or in music or in stone from his daily conduct, daily living. That demands the highest intelligence, highest harmony. To me the true artist is the man who has that harmony. He may express it on canvas, or he may talk, or he may paint; or he may not express it at all, he may feel it. But all this demands that exquisite poise, that intensity of awareness and therefore, his expression is not divorced from the daily continuity of living." The Alchemist teaches us to look for inspiration in all the corners of our lives.

Mastering the Alchemist at Work

Legend has it that Leo Burnett created the infamous Marlboro Man while using the principles of the Alchemist. Flipping through a magazine, he happened upon the image of an American cowboy. Burnett made the creative connection between the masculinity of the cowboy image and the Philip Morris cigarette assignment that recently came to his agency. Perhaps the cowboy could become the defining character for the cigarette. With this connection one of the most successful brands in history was born.

Knowing how to make connections to create inventive ideas is the powerful business skill of the Alchemist. Here's how the Alchemist principles can become your doorway to ideas at work.

DECIDE WHERE AND WHAT TO STEAL

Alchemists often get an inspiration for the direction of their business responsibilities by looking at other firms. They draw connections from other businesses and industries to find great ideas.

Millard "Mickey" Drexler, CEO of the GAP, drew upon an idea from the Coca-Cola annual report. The report mentioned Coke's strategy of ubiquity—being everywhere a thirsty person might be. Drexler made a creative connection. Perhaps this strategy could be the key to growing the GAP business. Perhaps the GAP should be everywhere someone might need clothes. Drexler now describes the GAP growth strategy as a strategy of ubiquity. The GAP seems right around almost every corner. He used the analogy of the Coke business to grow his own.

Obviously it's not enough just to have an analogy. You have to have the right analogy. Alchemists are consummate benchmarkers, always searching for the right case history, the right business story that will give them the idea they need.

David Stern, commissioner of the NBA, organized a small collection of teams and became an international business powerhouse. His creative impetus came through the principles of the Alchemist. He built the basketball association around the ideas of some leading consumer companies. "In the early years, Mr. Stern used organizations like Disney and McDonald's as his marketing role models, rather than Major League Baseball or the NFL."

Stern believed that the model for NBA success was a brand franchise, not a sport franchise. It was the ability to rally the fans around a brand image that would become the defining stroke of Stern's creative genius. Just as Wright brought together two dissimilar domains in his architecture, so Stern brought together two dissimilar elements, a basketball team and a brand, and found what was valuable in the connection.

Jeff is a client whose dominant creative skill was that of the Alchemist. A human resource manager for a large technology company, he was having trouble finding qualified candidates to fill slots within the firm. There was only a small handful of college graduates with the programming capabilities his firm needed. When he looked to the future, he projected his firm would be in this same position for some years to come. The typical recruiting techniques—going to colleges, using recruiters—wasn't going to be enough. How could he generate breakthrough recruiting ideas?

In typical Alchemist fashion, Jeff asked himself, "What do other organizations do to find talent?" Here he began a process of deciding where and what to steal. He made a list of nonprofits large and small, past and present. One organization he listed was the Presbyterian Church. He said, "I remembered the way churches in history typically found qualified candidates for ministers was to create their own school. That's how seminaries were born." Jeff realized he could create his own training program by affiliating with a nearby college. This began the training program that now provides his company a pipeline of technical talent for years to come.

Think of the Alchemist as the sociologist of industries. Alchemists keep their eyes open for what is happening around them. What's happening in biotech? Are there any similarities to what my industry is experiencing? What's happening in high-end retail? Are there any similarities to my industry? To my job? Andy Grove, former CEO of Intel, said one of his customers likened the microchip business to the fashion industry. "Andy, this is like the fashion business. We need something new."

Many marriages suffer from industry "silo thinking." We know our own industry better than a Wall Street analyst. We know the players, the competitive issues, what makes things tick. We are subject-matter experts. While this is what often makes us great, it is also what makes us weak. Silo thinking leads to insularity that prevents business genius. The only frame of reference becomes the view through our own industry—or worse yet, our own firm. To get to new ideas, you feel like Alice in Wonderland trying to squeeze through a very narrow looking glass.

But the Alchemist is the antidote to silo thinking. Alchemists are so interested in other fields that they are always bringing in new influences and challenging "the way we've always done things." They use their wide range of interests as a catalyst for fresh ideas. They are always drawing connections and their genius is their ability to choose a fertile analogy—the best model to borrow. While you don't have to steal the key like Raphael to get ideas, business artists are always ready to borrow them when they can.

You'll be happy to know that the Alchemists' skills are relatively easy to add to your imagination tool kit. Try this approach:

Become a student of other industries.

Pick an industry that captures your imagination—automotive? beauty care? online retailing? Track it for a while. What is happening? What trends are taking place? What competitive moves are being made? See what connections you can draw between that industry and yours.

STITCH TOGETHER WORK AND PLAY

We said earlier that Alchemists do not lead compartmentalized lives. This means their entire environment is a source of great work ideas. While gardening, while playing in the yard with the kids, while antiquing, Alchemists get brilliant inspirations.

There are few boundaries between Alchemists' creative spirit at work and creative spirit at home. A conversation at the hardware store reminds them how to improve the firm's customer service. The webbing of building materials on a construction site makes them think of new software programming paths. Like Bob Dylan, they are "influenced by everything and everybody."

Listen to a discussion about Bill Joy, the innovation guru at Sun Microsystems. "Joy finds revealing parallels to his work in just about everything he hears, sees, or reads. A man of prodigiously broad interests, he can talk knowledgeably about Meso-American art or cattle ranching or photography or stock market 'quant' theories. During a discussion of high-tech corporate culture . . . he dances deftly among references to Jungian psychology, the plays of Eugene O'Neill and the writing of G. I. Gurdjieff."

Joy uses his broad range of interests as a starting-off point for his ideas at work.

Here's how a teacher uses the magic of the Alchemist in her work. "One Saturday, my family went to an art exhibit at the Museum of Modern Art. A sculptor had created huge pieces of art from garbage. He recycled junk to create imaginary factories and machinelike contraptions. My seventh-graders are studying recyling in our science segment. I made the connection and realized I could have my students design their own sculptures from junk they collected. The art project was a tremendous hit with the students and they learned more than I could have ever imagined." Learn to use your own interests as a spark for ideas, a connection point between you and others at work.

Alchemists know that what interests them personally may well interest a larger audience. So Alchemists stay tuned to what gives them joy, intrigues them, thrills them. By staying on top of their interests they can be the first to recognize trends in their business or industry.

Sometimes we fall into a trap and see ourselves as separate and distinct from the customers we serve at work. We unintentionally highlight the differences between ourselves and our co-workers, customers, and clients. We have more education. They have more free time. We are prudent with our money. They have money to burn. They don't enjoy watching TV. We do.

But the Alchemist sees similarities and identifies the common ground between us and our markets. The Alchemist helps you remember how similar we are to each other and that when something is important to you, it may well be of interest to those around you. That connection can lead to ideas.

The team of Marcy Carsey and Tom Werner produced the hit comedy series *Roseanne*. When asked how they got the breakthrough idea for the show, they responded, "We basically sat back and asked, What's going on in our own lives? We work, we go home, we raise kids. We're not so different from anyone else." They connected their own lives to the lives of others and came up with the brilliant idea of the *Roseanne* show, which celebrated the honest joys and pains of the American family. What was of concern to them about their lives was also concerning others around them. When Alchemists find the courage to discover their personal interests and connect them to their work, their business genius burns.

To augment your Alchemist skills, consider mixing business with pleasure. Alchemists have a porous boundary between their personal life and work. They are driven by their passions. You will rarely see an Alchemist hang on to a job after the passion is gone.

Try these techniques to bring together work and play:

1. Inject some fun into work and some work into fun.

Get out of the office and visit customers. Take colleagues out to lunch. Ask a client to walk with you around the building. Figure out what you enjoy doing and bring it into your work.

Then while you're playing, keep your eyes open for analogies. Does the volleyball game remind you of a way to solve a communication problem? Does the shop window remind you of a better way to display your services? Let ideas pass fluidly between work and play.

2. Make a list of things in common between your life and your markets— your co-workers, your customers, your clients.

What are your new interests? Identify what seems exciting and fresh to you. Then ask yourself if your interests reflect a larger trend. Are you using your cell phone less? Hungering for more time with friends? Bored with TV? Maybe you are on the threshold of ideas that can change your firm and your work.

FIND INSPIRATION IN CONVERSATION

More than any other Face, Alchemists rely on the back and forth of dialogue for inspiration. The Alchemist finds it difficult to create in a personal vacuum. They prefer to bounce ideas off a group of colleagues—solicit the ideas of others and then shape their own.

Peter Lynch is the former manager of Fidelity's Magellan Fund. Lynch's job was to manage stock purchases that would yield the biggest returns for investors over time. Lynch purchased Hanes stock and the textiles firm developed a new product called L'eggs, a pantyhose sold in grocery stores. Soon a competitor came out with a similar product, called No nonsense. In an effort to determine whether to hold on to the Hanes stock, Lynch conducted some research. He purchased fifty pairs of L'eggs and No nonsense. He gave these pantyhose to his wife, her friends, his female colleagues. He asked them for their comments. Which pantyhose was the superior product? He found No nonsense didn't hold a candle to L'eggs. Lynch decided to hold on to the Hanes stock. Hanes turned out to be a big financial victory for Fidelity. Lynch used the casual research of conversation to shape his ideas.

It's easy to make the mistake that research has to be big, complicated, and technical, or that creative insights come from a regression analysis or a double-blind study. Alchemists research every day by listening to the interests of those closest to them. By assessing the personal interests of those around him, Lynch was able to make an important and valuable decision for the firm. Just like T. S. Eliot, Lynch solicited the ideas of others to make a breakthrough.

In addition to finding inspiration in conversation, Alchemists tend to be verbal in their creative style. They feel their ideas have more validity and are more concrete when they hear them expressed aloud. Alchemists tend to be "idea talkers."

Michelle is in the catering business, and when I met her she was looking forward to expanding her business. She knew she needed to hire additional staff to grow but was concerned about the business plan. Hiring new people would mean less money for her in the short term. But as she was able to take on more work, she could make more money for her firm in the long term.

As she considered the decision before her, she took a Saturday off to do some chores around the house. While taking out the garbage, she struck up a conversation with her neighbor, who was gardening. The caterer asked what else the gardener had left to do in the yard. "All I have to do yet is finish pruning the roses. It always amazes me that it's only when I cut the roses back that they begin to bloom." Michelle said, "That's when I knew I had to take the step and hire the staff for my catering business. If I wasn't willing to 'prune' my income, there was no way for the business to bloom. That was the beginning of the firm's real growth." It is conversation that becomes the creative fuel for the Alchemist.

Ideas through conversation can happen across geographic and cultural boundaries. For Alchemists, it is possible for them to make connections with other cultures to develop breakthrough ideas. Howard Behar, the former head of Starbucks International, credits the growth of the firm across cultures to their efforts to connect domains. "Starbucks set out to be a bridge among people and among cultures, not to sell more coffee." By emphasizing the learning that goes both ways across a bridge, Starbucks was able to accommodate and influence the cultures and so successfully expand the company internationally.

Knowledge sharing is another type of conversation Alchemists enjoy. At British Petroleum, CEO John Browne admits, "We have found that our peoples' ability to combine and apply technologies—not the technologies themselves—is often what gives us an advantage." Alchemists know what information is valuable, and they are good at mixing the critical pieces of knowledge and reapplying them in different areas.

Try these ways to find inspiration in conversation:

1. Institute a "roundtable" every week.

In a roundtable meeting, each member has forty-five seconds—a sound bite—to explain their hot issues to others, what they are working on, what interests them. If someone else becomes engaged in that idea, they can follow up and learn more from the team member. If you can learn about a world news event in forty-five seconds, you can learn a little about what a colleague is up to.

2. Keep a business journal.

You can jot down ideas from your conversations with others and use the writing process as a way to "converse" with your own ideas. When someone shares an intriguing business idea, write it down. You can thoroughly study it and analyze it better when you've committed it to the written page. Journaling helps you to record thoughts for future reflection. For more on journaling, check out page 88.

USE ANALOGIES AS BRIDGES TO IDEAS

Alchemists are brilliant analogy makers. You've worked with these folks before. They say things like, "That reminds me of . . ." or, "It's like a . . ." In fact they can even drive you crazy with their analogies. But it is the analogy that becomes the pattern or the stamp to make the new idea. Alchemists can even design new products and services through analogies.

Bill Bowerman was an Oregon track coach and one of the initiators of the jogging movement in America. It was clear to him that there was a need for comfortable and durable jogging shoes. Traditional sneakers wore out quickly and weren't designed for the wear and tear of jogging. Bowerman was working in the kitchen one day and saw the open waffle iron. He made the connection between the pattern of the waffle and his need for a comfortable shoe. The waffle iron was the analogy for the bottom of the jogging shoe. He filled the waffle iron with modeling clay and began designing what would become the first Nike shoe.

Or how about the story of George Eastman, the creator of the popular Kodak camera? Prior to the launch of the Kodak camera in 1888, all film had to be loaded on individual plates. Eastman made the connection between a rolling window shade and the way film could pass the lens of the camera. The rolling window shade became the analogy that drove the invention of the new camera.

You can often identify Alchemists by the sports analogies they use. "These last quarter sales are like making the three pointer at the buzzer" or, "This new service is so easy, it's like a two-foot putt." But what makes the Alchemist a business artist is that the analogy itself often leads to great ideas.

To hone your Alchemist skills, watch the Alchemists around you. They describe their ideas in terms of something else. You can learn a lot by studying their natural benchmarking—their scanning for good ideas. When they love a good idea, ask them where they got it. Was it from something they read? A play they saw? When you begin to understand how the analogies lead to ideas you'll realize how easily you can add it to your creative portfolio. The Alchemist is waiting to be your inspiration.

Try this:

Identify friends who are Alchemists and watch them at work.

Notice how Alchemists use analogies as a means to ideas. Let them know you are going to build this skill and ask their assistance. Practice with them. Look for similarities and find ideas.

Here is a summary of the key business principles of the Alchemist:

1. Decide where and what to steal: Become a student of other industries.
2. Stitch together work and play: Use your interests outside work as inspiration.
3. Find inspiration in conversation: Expect ideas from dialogue with others.

4. Use analogies as bridges to ideas: Pay attention to the similarities around you.

Alchemists and Teams

Alchemists have reputations as creative leaders. They garner respect because of their wealth of ideas and intuitive leaps from compelling analogies. Their connection process is often fairly obvious to those around them and is very valued.

Think of your team members who use analogies to solve problems. A manager at an information systems company compared his client's software problems to the spread of a Yosemite brush fire. His team began to talk about the problem using the analogy. They used ways to extinguish fire to search for creative solutions to the problem. They could deny the fire oxygen—shut the entire system down and make repairs. Or they could burn around the edges to contain the fire by denying them fuel. This meant shutting down part of the system that harbored the worst of the problems even if it meant taking more time. The analogy helped the team determine alternative courses of action. Alchemists use this principle of analogy in group creative process.

Alchemists like the "bounce and catch" of creative dialogue. If Observers are more introverted, Alchemists tend to be more extroverted. They usually come to ideas rapidly and love the team experience of ideation. As creative leaders, Alchemists need to remember that others may use a more internal creative style. They have to wait for others to create in their own time and in their own style. When Alchemists master the other skills, they can evoke the highest creative content from others.

Because Alchemists' use of analogies often makes them powerful communicators, they are thought leaders in organizations. You can find them in all disciplines of an organization, but pockets are found in sales and other areas that require stellar communication skills.

They love working in creative group environments because the imaginations of others fuel their connections. This means Alchemists need to be intentional about changing their team environments often. They burn this fuel over time and then need fresh team experiences to spark ideas.

AN ALCHEMIST TEAM EXERCISE

Try an exercise called "That reminds me of . . ." First, outline the issue you'd like to discuss or have a "task headline" for the meeting, then try to generate a list of analogous situations. Let's say you're a paper manufacturer trying to come up with a better way to identify quality sales leads. Each member might come up with a "That reminds me of . . ." analogy. Members start out by filling in the sentence, "People who buy paper in large quantities remind me of . . ." Answers might be: ". . . the people who buy energy in large quantities from electric companies" or, "investment bankers who identify quality start-ups to fund" or, "mortgage lenders who sell lines of credit to companies with large sales volume."

Once a list is generated, go back and share what you know about these processes of identifying sales leads. Perhaps you know mortgage lenders have a dedicated staff to search qualified leads on a full-time basis. Or investment bankers spend time informally networking in high-tech circles. Or electric companies use computer modeling techniques. You may need to get more information on some analogies, but once you've explored the options, you will spark electric ideas for you and your firm.

Alchemist Pitfalls to Avoid

Because Alchemists perceive similarities in an analogy, they have to work to be sure they haven't minimized the differences. They should always be clear about the disconnects that exist within an analogy.

Alchemists usually have a large quantity of ideas. They are constantly sparking connections. Consequently their rapid-fire ideas can become overwhelming to those around them. Alchemists need to screen ideas to be sure they are sharing the best ones. They do well to focus and champion a few key ideas.

Alchemists navigate their imagination by going first to analogies. Yet it's possible that there are no analogous situations and that the dilemma is entirely new to your experience. Be willing to drop the Alchemist tool and move to the next one. Try to fish in another river for ideas.

The Five·Five Faces of Genius Summary

	THE SEER	THE OBSERVER	THE ALCHEMIST	THE FOOL	THE SAGE
The Creative Power Principle	The Power to Image	The Power to Notice Detail	The Power to Connect Domains	The Power to Celebrate Weakness	The Power to Simplify
Key Creative Skill	Visualization	Ideas from the collection of detail Curiosity	Ideas from connection		
Easy Way to Remember the Face	See it	Notice it	Mix it		
Benefit to Teams	Vision for future Test possible outcomes	Conceptual thinking rooted in real issues	Insights through analogies		
Pitfalls	Needs to combine Seer with other Faces	Needs to collect a variety of details	Watch for weaknesses in analogy		

Exercises

Here are some ways to begin to master the Alchemist in your current work responsibilities. Watch for electric ideas as you make connections.

The industry that is most similar to my business

is _____

because _____

Three things my business can learn from that industry include:

1)

2)

3)

An industry that has little in common with my business

is _____

because _____

Three things my business can learn from that industry include:

1)

2)

3)

An industry that really intrigues me

is _____

because _____

Three things my business can learn from that industry include:

1)

2)

3)

WORK DIFFERENTLY

Starting a Business Salon

Salons are small gatherings in which people intentionally get together for the joy of conversation. No agenda, no goals, no outcomes. Just thinking together. Salons have been in existence since Roman times but peaked in popularity in seventeenth-century Paris. Groups of artists, poets, thinkers, and patrons regularly got together to talk about ideas. From political theories to arts and literature, these salons were often attended by some of the most influential thinkers of the time. The salon sometimes became the nexus of great cultural movements. They led the culture in times of great change.

A business salon can be a place of enlightenment and change for you and your team. A group of business folks simply gathered to converse about what's going on in the world can be the impetus for unusual ideas and great innovation. No ostensible "goal," just consciousness raising about culture, ideas, and society.

Business folks live by the belief that there should be "an objective" or "an outcome" to every meeting. But in a business renaissance spending time on tightly defined objectives narrows the range of creative possibilities too soon. Managers (and companies) that fail tend to do so because they have ignored larger forces of change that existed beyond the accepted boundaries of the firm—beyond their defined "objectives."

Create a diverse group of folks. Don't limit the group to just your business team. Include those who are interested in artistry in any field. Start to talk about what you've seen lately, what you've read lately. What interests you? What do you think the next new trends are? What are some of the horizons of change? What you and your colleagues come up with will surprise you. The salon can feed the soul of the business artist.

In our workshops we practice the Business Salon. We ask participants to bring in an article or book that they have found interesting recently. Each person shares the thought or concept with the others. Our theory is that if our participants find it interesting, the idea may be a beacon or a guidepost to what is happening in the larger culture around us. As we go around the circle, we try to draw implications for how this idea reflects what's going on in the larger society. How does this represent our world? Does it have any reflection on our markets?

For example, one client brought the book *Tuesdays with Morrie*. This is a book that shares a student's conversations with a former teacher as the teacher lay dying. The participant found the story related the struggle with death, life, and memory. We then began to talk about implications for the larger society. How could these themes of death and meaning in life be interesting to our markets?

We talked about the recent increased interest in spirituality, and that in business we often overlook the spiritual needs of our customer. The conversation led in many different directions. The participant had the insight that his communication with customers lacked a human connection that could help the firm.

Salons give colleagues and teams the chance to bat around ideas without the pressure of some definitive "next steps." It allows for dreaming, for fresh thinking, and for the breezes of innovation to blow. As Clarissa Pinkola Estés says, "Playing aimlessly with a goal" is the hallmark of creativity.

Learning Business Journaling from the Alchemist

I once lost my electronic organizer on a plane and my world crumbled. Our business calendars master us. Our schedule drags us through our day and dominates our life at work.

But imagine for a moment being as passionate about managing our ideas as we are about managing our calendar. Imagine if we kept track of our ideas with the same fervency that we kept track of our schedule. What if we kept a book to our breast that included our business inspirations, our random thoughts, and our best ideas in addition to our meeting planner?

Artists and scientists are ready for the muse to speak at any time. Most carry a sketchpad or a notebook to record their thoughts. They use this as a journal of innovation, making sure no idea is lost.

Edison carried a pocket notebook. He kept notes on his wide range of interests, from the qualities of metals to the transmission of electricity. Leonardo da Vinci kept a vast notebook of his ideas and inspirations. Richard Feynman created a journal entitled "Things I Don't Know About."

Can you image how useful it would be to have a journal called "Things I Don't Know About the Business," where you could record questions? You'd have the ingredients for some genius ideas.

The Alchemist teaches us to look for inspiration from all parts of our lives. This means journaling is a valuable tool for the business artist. A journal is a place to record your ruminations, your musings, your ideas that you don't want to lose. Say when you have an inspiration at a customer meeting and think you will hold on to it, but it gets lost in the next task. The idea will be lost. Our short-term memories can hang on to only so much information.

Journaling is a way to put imagination before implementation. Business artists keep a journal close at hand to follow the arc of their business ideas. The journal can also serve as a history that is valuable when you are planning for the future.

Carry your journal with your calendar. Use it in meetings to chronicle your questions and record your ideas. Pull it out when you are reaching for radiant ideas.

It's said that the gods give instructions while you sleep. Instead of a journal, some folks keep a note pad or tape recorder by their bed so they can record their ideas when they reveal themselves in the night. Only when you record do you give the ideas the honor they deserve. It's the ideas we do something about that count.

4. THE FOOL

THE POWER TO CELEBRATE WEAKNESS

"Living is a form of not being sure, not knowing what next or how. The artist never entirely knows. We guess. We take leap after leap in the dark."
—AGNES DE MILLE

The story is e-commerce history. In 1994 Jeff Bezos was working on Wall Street. When he read that Internet use was increasing 2,300 percent per year, he wondered how he could ride the wave. After creating a list of products that could be sold online, he picked books. He quit his job, hired a moving van, and said to the movers, "Head west and call us tomorrow." Writing his business plan in the car on the way to Seattle, Bezos started Amazon.com, the company that revolutionized retailing.

In retrospect, Bezos's guts seem savvy. Today we see clearly how he capitalized on the Internet before it became mainstream and created opportunity in the business renaissance. But at the time he decided to take the risk, it seemed absurd. That's why the story captures our imagination. Jeff Bezos used a Fool skill. He pursued the absurd notion and won.

You may think, "Isn't the Fool a negative title? I mean, does anybody want their creative style to be known as the Fool?" Surprisingly, if your creative style is that of the Fool, you see the distinction as a badge of honor. Fools almost immediately recognize themselves and say, "That's me. That's me!" They are thrilled to find that their skill is recognized and appreciated.

Suspend any disbelief you may have that the Fool is a fool. Fools are rare in corporations, yet they are highly valuable. When you begin to tap into the Fool within, you will find a myriad of new tools you probably never knew existed.

The Fool is the most complex of the Five Faces of Genius and perhaps requires the most mental firepower. There are three related skills of the Fool:

1. Fools excel at inversion.
2. Fools use aburdity to break through.
3. Fools have unending perseverance.

Each of these techniques will open new pathways to your genius. They will usher you into the new frontiers of the business renaissance.

The Creative Genius of the Fool: Find Ideas Lurking Under Weakness

Steve Martin was a presenter at the Academy Awards. He opened the envelope to share the winner. Instead of saying, "And the winner is . . . ," he drew laughs from the crowd by saying, "And the loser isn't . . ."

FOOLS EXCEL AT INVERSION

Fools love to reverse expectations, find the surprise, and in so doing create breakthrough ideas. Inversion is a tried-and-true principle implemented by creative genius. Consider the impressionists of European painting in the late 1800s. Artists like Monet, Manet, Renoir, and Degas were born at a time when representationalism was the trend in painting. Elaborate details, smooth surfaces, and highly finished canvases were in vogue. Then photography was born and challenged that traditional definition of fine art. Some artists had a competitive spirit and asked, "What now is the role of painting?"

The impressionists broke the status quo. Rather than worry about accurate representations, they painted their *impressions* of conventional reality. Impressionists used small strokes and bright patches of contrasting color to create an illusion of what the naked eye saw. Their revolution inverted the nature of the craft and turned around our expectations of what painting was all about.

How about the character of the fool in Shakespeare's *King Lear*? Lear was about to be betrayed by his daughters, yet he didn't want to admit to himself a threat was near. It was too painful a truth. But on Lear's court sat the fool. In Greek tragedy, the fool has no status within the court but cannot keep the real truth to himself. The fool leaks the truth to Lear. Yes, two of his three daughters were going to betray him. He tells Lear the dark side of Lear's consciousness. The heart of the story is the risk and reward of love. The Fool uses inversion to speak the full truth.

Fools see both sides of the story, and they know which is the hidden truth. Fools flip around your expectations. They make you laugh by pointing out a vulnerability or showing a weakness.

When you embrace the skills of the Fool, you'll learn how to dig below the surface and find the truth within complicated situations. You'll be able to reveal the underside of what's really going on—with your co-workers, your customers, and your business. The Fool can find what is hidden. Inversion reveals the less obvious.

ABSURDITY AS BREAKTHROUGH

Fools like to take a notion and push it to its extreme conclusion. They make sense through nonsense. Claes Oldenburg is a pop artist whose work features sculptures of everyday objects. Oldenburg created a giant ice bag that was more than fifteen feet high and eighteen feet wide. The ice bag had a motor and it moved. Oldenburg celebrated the ordinary. His genius is making you consider the power of the mundane through an absurdity.

Fools make sense through the nonsense of accidents. They take what seems at first to be a disaster and find ways to fix it. Accidents become the inroads into something new that may not have existed—new ideas for working together or even a new idea to grow your business. As one client encourages his people, "I tell folks to fail forward." That is, use your accidents and mistakes as a field for learning.

Sometimes you have to wonder if Fools don't create the accident just to see the creative result! Charles Goodyear spilled rubber and sulfur on the stove and created vulcanized rubber. Sir Alexander Fleming discovered penicillin when he accidentally noticed a stray spore on the edge of a petri dish. Fools use accidents, however absurd, as a means to discovery.

It's worth asking yourself the question, "What do I do when I make a mistake?" Common responses are, "I try to forget it and move ahead." Or, "I try to cover it up so no one will notice." Especially in a corporate environment, mistakes are rarely rewarded. But when we value our contributions at work and get our job satisfaction from creative growth, we become more interested in our errors and our accidents. They become something to redeem.

The musician Brian Eno said, "Honor your errors as hidden intentions." For the Fool errors are worthwhile explorations. Something valuable is hidden in the folds of an error. Examining failure becomes a treasure hunt. When we examine failure we find knowledge about ourselves we can find no other place.

The psychiatrist Charles Johnstone tells us, "Traditional American quilts often have a 'lucky square,' one with a mistake, so the quilt can breathe and be alive. Navajo weaving similarly includes an 'error,' and ritual sand paintings a break in the circle through which the spirits can pass." While we may try to hide our errors, Fools honor them.

Fools also know garbage is somehow grist for the idea mill. For you and me it may seem absurd to ponder garbage, but the Fool uses it to break through the status quo. Leftovers are holy.

An art professor in college asked us to create "pinch pots." Since most of us mastered these in elementary school, the class wondered what was up his sleeve. Nevertheless, each student rolled perfect logs of clay, measured them with precision, and artfully constructed pots. As the class continued, he instructed us to put our pots aside. He said, "Now, look at your scrap pile. Let's find the real art of this exercise—the garbage that has been left over." We used what we had discarded as the ingredients for a new piece of art. We prepared our pile of clay scraps to be fired in the kiln. The teacher was using the skill of the Fool—creating something new by redeeming the garbage.

The mythologist Joseph Campbell said, "Out of rot comes life." What is rotten and decayed often has the potential to reignite and reinvigorate. In weakness is some potential for creative strength. Fools find ideas lurking under weakness.

You can use the garbage, the accidents, and the leftovers as power to move ahead. The Fool will help propel you into new ideas and newfound creative energy.

UNENDING PERSEVERANCE

What we perceive to be opposites are often related and the Fool intimately knows this. That's why inversion works. And absurdity. The genius of the Fool is that he surprises us by revealing both sides of a truth. Fools are truth tellers.

Because they are so convinced of their truth, Fools are on a mission called creativity. Fools persevere. I'm sure you've met these folks. They risk and fail; they are courageous in their pursuit of truth.

The book *Longitude* tells the story of John Harrison, who invented a clock to navigate the seas. Prior to Harrison's clock, the maritime world used celestial bearings to calculate the longitude of their location. Harrison was convinced that his timepiece would be the invention that would help the English government navigate the Atlantic with accuracy and precision. Harrison devoted his entire life to the development of this clock. From 1730 to 1770 Harrison created five different timepieces. Through intense frustration, political strife, and competition from other inventors, he persevered to create the timepiece that revolutionized sea travel. He said, "I think I may be bold to say, that there is neither any other Mechanical or Mathematical thing in all the World, that is more beautiful or curious in texture than this watch or Timekeeper for the Longitude . . . and I heartily thank Almighty God that I have lived so long, as in some measure to complete it." The perseverance of the Fool led to his breakthrough.

The reasons Fools can perservere is that they have a passion for what is right. They believe it in their soul. When you touch your passion, it gives you the drive to continue to press on and the power to persist.

Mathematician Andrew Wiles is credited for solving one of the greatest mathematical mysteries of all time, Fermat's last theorem. Pierre Fermat was a seventeenth-century French scholar who jotted a mathematical equation in a margin of his notes. For hundreds of years the math community tried to solve the theorem. Andrew Wiles, a professor at Princeton, decided to take the solution on as a personal challenge. For seven years Wiles worked secretly on solving the proof. After these long years of arduous labor he thought he had the answer. Wiles revealed his research to academic peers and was received with great celebration.

But after scrutiny, a colleague determined there was a flaw in Wiles's proof. Wiles returned to his study to work the theorem once again. After another year of study he felt he was losing his struggle. Dejected and tired, Wiles contemplated giving up. Finally, he decided to go back to the proof and "take one last look at his proof before chucking it all and abandoning all hope to prove Fermat's Last Theorem." After all this time, Wiles wanted to explain to himself why he failed. Like a coroner identifying the cause of death, Wiles culled through the proof once again. As he searched for a flaw, he found the inconsistency that led him to the solution of the theorem. His perseverance led him through the valley of discovery.

Now you and I might just give up after a few months of hard work. But Wiles keeps at it. He knows he is close. He knows he has a hold of some original thread. He keeps pulling. Keeps trying. When we hold our passion in front of us and don't let go, we find the genius idea.

Claude Monet painted the same subjects over and over and over again. He painted haystacks in the field in a late summer day. He painted them with snow. He painted haystacks when the sun was low in the sky. He painted them in broad daylight. His perseverance led to some of the most sensitive interpretations in painting.

Those who create need to be able to persevere. They need to be so convinced they are on a path of truth that they will follow no matter what. Clarissa Pinkola Estés says that a creative genius has the power to be in the creative tension and "stand it." Stand the internal pressure you put on yourself. Stand the external pressure others put on you. Stand the chaos.

So inversion, absurdity, and perseverance make up the central nervous system of the Fool. These are the three skills collected under the headline of celebrating weakness. Fools see weakness and understand its topography. They love the dark side. They find a way to turn weakness around, power through it, and help us respect its value.

Take these principles and hold them to your heart. They are counterintuitive for most of us. Counter to what we might naturally do. But when you explore the territory of the Fool, you're sure to find the unexpected idea and find yourself delighted.

Let's see how these notions of celebrating weakness bring us closer to becoming business artists.

Mastering the Fool at Work

When Sam Walton, founder of Wal-Mart, began expanding his drugstore chain, inversion inspired his breakthrough. Instead of building warehouses near his retail outlets, he did the opposite of conventional wisdom. He built retail outlets near his warehouses. Walton systematically placed warehouses where he could easily serve the greatest number of retail stores. Walton took the wisdom of the retailing industry and turned it upside down.

In the past, retailers put stores in locations that had lots of people around. Now, instead of paying money to ship items from one distant location to another, Walton had everything he needed at his stores quickly and easily. What better way to reduce his costs? He could dominate by logistics. Walton inverted his response to the industry and became the leading discount retailer in the nation. Like the impressionist painters, Walton turned the status quo around and surprised the world with a breakthrough.

But don't let Walton's example of business genius intimidate you. The Fool tools are quickly added to your portfolio of skills. You'll see immediate results within your work. Clients tell me the Fool's skills are some they never considered before and are easily incorporated into their thinking about business.

I mentioned that mastering the skills of the Fool requires a high degree of mental firepower. You may want to consider breaking up the Fool tools and tackling them one at a time. For example, you may find inversion easier to take on than perseverance. Or you can learn to invert an idea and look at opposite solutions or that absurdity is a less daunting task than inversion. Experiment with the different sides of the Fool. See what fits best for you.

RUN THE OTHER WAY

When facing a challenge, the Fool's first instinct is to invert. They find a way out of sticky problems by trying the "upside down" approach. If they are caught in a bind, they will dream about the opposite situation to create a solution.

And consider the genius of Oprah Winfrey. As Oprah shaped her talk show over the years, the status quo became the raucous banter of Jerry Springer. Oprah chose the opposite tack. Instead of playing off the weaknesses of people, Oprah focused on their strengths. She featured the heroes of today—the women who were great mothers, the fathers who stayed home with children, the people who helped the sick. She believed people should read books, so she started her widely successful book club. She supported the spiritual side of her audience with everyday rituals for faith. Her inverted approach to television programming has won her consistent ratings and the hearts of millions. Inversion. Breaking convention. Turning things upside down. This is the first principle of the Fool.

Most clients find inversion a tactic they never thought to apply to their business limitations. Ask yourself, What are the constraints? What are the boundaries? The rules? Then try to invert them. What if the opposite were true? You're certain to find some unlikely ideas that few others have considered.

Rita worked for a large insurance agency. In charge of communicating new insurance products to the agents of the firms, she was responsible for educating the agents about the terms of all the new insurance·products. Rita became increasingly busy fielding calls from agents around the world asking questions about the details of the plans. She was becoming overwhelmed. Her first inclination was to try and meet every request, but then she decided to put some Fool tools to work.

What if she turned it upside down? What if she decided *not* to handle all the requests? What ideas could she generate? Rita created a telephone menu of options that agents could access to get answers to frequently asked questions, and she left her name as the final contact. She explained the extra costs involved to her boss by saying, "I know you wouldn't want me to waste my time and you would want me to concentrate on the most important projects in front of me." Rita proved herself a thought leader by breaking the conventional wisdom of finishing all the work there is to do.

Millard "Mickey" Drexler, CEO of the GAP, has a strange management practice. He roams the halls of the corporate office, saying to employees, "Think negative five comp." What does he mean by this odd expression? GAP business is booming. In fact, comparable stores' sales are up.

Drexler wants his people to *think* as if store sales are down 5 percent. He wants his people to imagine a different mental landscape. It's his way of improving the staff's business imagination. Imagine things are bad and you'll generate the ideas needed for what inevitably lies ahead—competition. When you run the other way of conventional reality, you find genius.

Once you become aware of the power of inversion, you'll start to notice it everywhere. You'll see how it leads to breakthrough. You'll see your colleagues using it. You'll see the competition using it. You'll learn to use it.

This inversion approach can be literal. Playtex Products makes a cute little "sippy cup" for kids. Sippy cups are plastic cups with tight caps shaped with a spout for little folks. Playtex put the product on the market, but it didn't sell well. So they reconsidered. Playtex decided to show the cup inverted in the package. Put it upside down. Mimic its leakproof qualities. Sales skyrocketed and the sippy cup became one of Playtex's hottest-selling products. The Fool breaks through barriers by inverting the status quo.

To immediately augment your Fool's skills try these approaches:

1. Choose a problem task and ask yourself: "How could I turn it upside down?"

Think of the opposite of what you want to happen. What do you uncover? How about the silliest solution or the craziest idea? Sometimes the counterintuitive ideas are most fruitful. You'll begin to find unexpected solutions through inversion.

2. Study a comedian.

I asked one of the best business professors at a leading MBA program where he learned his creative style. He said he studied Chevy Chase. Choose a comedian and study his style. Learn what makes that comedian funny. Why do they make you laugh?

REACH OVER THE TOP

Business artists master absurdity as well as inversion. Absurdity is a little more subtle to recognize but every bit as powerful an innovation tool. Like the big ice-bag sculpture of Claes Oldenburg, Fools generate ideas by taking a notion and pushing it to the extreme.

Some exclusive hotels are using a strategy of absurdity. When other hotels are focusing on superior customer service—meeting your every need, being highly polite—others, like the Paramount Hotel in New York

City, take a different tack. They want to be seen as the trendiest hotel in town. They want to be known for their clientele. They intend that you will come to the Paramount because you may run into Brad Pitt, not because of the service. To do that they take a different approach. The hotel is over the top. The lobby looks like a modern art museum. It's expensive. The rooms are tiny. As Nancy Keates asks in her *Wall Street Journal* article: "Is This a Hotel Room or a Broom Closet?" It's absurdity at work.

Sometimes the absurd approach can be foolish, like childhood fun. There is a popular restaurant in Chicago where the wait staff pretends to be rude. It is an old-fashioned fifties diner, and the staff asks for your order with "What do ya want?" The waitress sits down next to you to "get a load off " her feet. They often rush you to get out. It's loads of fun. Their slogan is "Eat at Ed's. Eat and get out."

I tell clients instead of step change, create sea change. In times of change don't strive for ideas that make things a little bit better. Strive for ideas that make things completely different. The Fool principles help to stimulate those ideas that launch into the "completely different" category.

David, an information technology consultant for a large consulting firm, was hired by an equipment manufacturing company to reconfigure their information system and link the entry of the order to the sales organization. That way the sales team would have immediate knowledge of when the equipment had been finally shipped to customers.

Unfortunately, once David started the project, a management reorganization started at the equipment manufacturer. No one was quite sure who was on first base and what they ultimately wanted from the information system. David saw this as a red flag. He knew that to get the technology to do the best job for the firm, he was going to need to have the right management in place with the right frame of mind. "I didn't want to sell them something they didn't need."

David used the tools of the Fool to create an idea. He pursued an absurd move. He decided to resign the job. He explained that it wasn't in the manufacturing firm's best interest nor in his to continue. This move made such a big impact on the leadership of the company that they offered his firm the entire project—to handle the technology assignment *and* the reorganization of the company.

As "professionals" we often screen the absurd from our list of possibilities. We want to make sure our recommendations, our ideas, are realistic.

But it is often the case that what is realistic is boring, staid, expected. When you begin to be comfortable with absurdity and know when to use it, you'll find lots of opportunities to break through and lead.

Brazilian entrepreneur Ricardo Semler tells the story of his company, Semco. Semco is a manufacturing firm that produces everything from high-capacity dishwashers to air-conditioners. Semco has grown their revenue, profitability, and productivity by staggering numbers in the midst of recession, inflation, and unstable national economic policy. What was Semler's philosophy that led to Semco's great success?

Semler utilized the tools of the Fool. He runs the firm in such a way that from the outside it seems absurd. He gave factory workers the ability to set their own production quotas, and the workers set their own schedules to meet those quotas. Workers help redesign the products they make and influence how they are marketed. Semler even instituted a democratic system for large corporate decisions, like whether or not to buy another company.

Semco has no dress code, no corporate perks, no organization chart with fancy titles. There are no receptionists or personal assistants. Everyone answers their own phone and does their own paperwork. The financial record of the company is open to anyone who wants to look. They even trained the staff, including custodians, to read financial reports. And you may think this is truly absurd: workers set their own salary. Semler took the concept of participatory management and pushed it to its extreme.

Keep your antennae tuned to the unexpected, the wild, the spontaneous. When you open yourself to the foolish, you find your business genius within.

To begin to invite the absurd, try this:

Take the comic's approach.

Ask yourself how to approach a problem you face with a sense of humor. If you created some absurd solutions, how might you solve it? You'll have a wealth of new ideas.

PERSEVERE, PERSEVERE, AND PERSEVERE AGAIN

The last prong of the Fool is perseverance. Risking and trying. Risking again and trying again. Business annals are full of stories of Fools. Those who followed their truth even in the midst of failure.

Don Fisher, chairman and founder of the GAP, started the store in 1969. He has been so successful that few of us realize he had huge failures along the way. Ever hear of Ralph Lauren Western wear? Fisher had to write off $14 million for that "failure." He started Pottery Barn and found that business too different from the GAP to adequately manage both. Fisher had to write off $14 million once again. He said, "I never thought I'd make fourteen million dollars in my whole life, much less be able to write it off twice!" Success is punctuated by failures. But the Fool is undaunted. The Fool risks and fails and risks and fails. And waits to succeed.

Even in the face of turmoil, they persist. Like Wiles trying to solve Fermat's last theorem, the Fool keeps on keeping on. You can find the power to make your ideas happen.

Dave Packard, cofounder of Hewlett-Packard, describes how companies need the "maverick" among the group, the one that persists even when internal political obstacles are present.

One engineer in their oscilloscope technology lab, Charles "Chuck" House, was instructed by his management to stop developing the display monitor he was working on. Management felt there was little potential for its success. The "management" in this case even included Dave Packard. House decided to go on vacation to California and while he was there showed the prototype to potential customers. He got customer feedback on the monitor—what needed to be improved and what they liked. He continued with his work in spite of the request from management to stop. When the powers that be heard of the customers' excitement for the product, the monitor was rushed to production. HP sold more than seventeen thousand display monitors totaling $35 million in revenue for the company.

Now many of us feel this was a gutsy guy. He broke the rules. And we imagine ourselves in his shoes and wonder if we ever would have what it takes to keep pressing. But Fools feel as if they were not doing their job *unless* they are breaking the barriers. A business artist I know who characterizes himself a Fool keeps a fool playing card by his desk. He describes his job as "an opportunity to be a rebel and have fun." This is his core statement about what drives him to do the work he does.

I love this story of perserverence: Many of us have enjoyed a Starbucks Frappuccino. But we would never have had that pleasure if not for the creative genius of Dina Campion. Campion was a district manager for a group of Starbucks stores in Southern California. Some customers were coming in and asking for a blended cold coffee drink, and local managers had to turn them away because Starbucks had nothing to offer. Campion decided to spearhead the idea of a Starbucks frozen coffee drink. Campion found an ally in Starbucks who knew the needs of the California market. Together they blended their own frozen drink and started to sell it at one of her stores, all without asking permission. She felt this new product was a necessity. So she went up the ladder trying to get the research department to join the game and capture management approval.

Finally, the idea got to the CEO, Howard Schultz. He didn't like it. The frozen coffee drink was outside Starbucks' specialty of brewed coffee. It required new machinery in the store. But Schultz reluctantly gave permission for more testing. Campion persisted. While new prototypes were being developed, Campion found another ally at an even higher level in the organization, and after more hounding, Schultz gave in. In the first full year on the market, Frappuccino accounted for nearly 7 percent of Starbucks' total revenue. Schultz now calls Frappuccino the "best mistake I didn't make."

Fools operate on guts. They feed on instinct. It's as if they have a truth-telling meter. When they get close to what they see is a great idea, the meter starts quivering. More than any other face of genius, they follow their intuition. When they believe something is right, they do it, even if they fail. As Steve Jobs points out: "Pick something you really care about, then you just do it." What do you really care about at work? Do it.

When you're learning to master the Fool, a good rule of thumb: Don't give up too early. When you have an idea that you love, continue to push. Find a way to shove the idea uphill. Sometimes Fools succeed simply because they refuse to give up. Even when it seems realistic to quit, Fools keep trying. Force yourself to go an extra round. If you truly believe in your idea, fight for it.

The Fool skill of persevering through challenges may feel awkward to you as a newcomer. We've all known a Fool who has overrelied on pushing ideas and tired us, so we become wary of the principle. We ask ourselves, "How hard do I push? For how long?" Even though this skill of the Fool may seem unusual to you, it can be a very valuable first tool for invention. Most managers don't persevere enough. So even if you overcorrect and seemingly press too hard, it will probably not be perceived as strongly as you think. So try to tackle the perseverance of Fool early. You'll see some remarkable creative results.

Go at it again.

Think of a solution you've had to a problem that hasn't been accepted or approved by those in charge. Consider forwarding the idea *one more time*. Do they really know how passionate you are about it?

CELEBRATE FAILURE AND FIND SUCCESS

Not every risk that the Fool takes results in success. Failure is the opposite side of risk. They are inextricably tied and so the Fool knows to even celebrate the failure.

In the early 1990s, NBC was beginning to recognize the depth of the struggle that cable channels would pose to networks. Carrying the Olympics broadcast offered NBC a unique ability to boost network viewership. Tom Roger, a top executive at NBC, championed an entirely new idea to promote the Olympics on NBC and generate more revenue. The concept was called TripleCast. Viewers could buy additional coverage of games on three separate stations on a pay-per-view basis. Instead of merely watching the same Olympic coverage everyone else was watching, consumers could select their favorite sporting events. It was an act of innovation many saw as an industry breakthrough.

The problem was it failed. TripleCast lost NBC around $100 million. The managers who worked around Tom Roger expected him to lose his job. We all know the corporate practice of linking failure to individuals and then firing them. But something unexpected happened. Roger was promoted and given even more responsibility. Those within the organization felt the company was advocating for innovation. Kenneth Bronfin, a colleague, later said, "NBC sent a clear message that Tom was being rewarded for risk taking."

Risk taking is the underpinning of the Fool's way. Whether inverting conventional wisdom, pushing a notion to the absurd conclusion, or persevering, risk taking is central to each. As Shakespeare said in *As You Like It*, "The wise man knows himself to be a fool." Fools know that if they haven't risked and failed, they haven't truly tried.

Most successful managers risk and fail once. It's too painful to continue risking. We figure we must conform to the organization or die. Better to round off the edges and follow the culture. Adapt. It's a lot easier. But the Fool teaches us that it is more painful at times to compromise. In a business renaissance, avoiding failure will assuredly lead to failure.

Risk taking means making friends with failure. Steve is a manager of a national real estate brokerage firm. He and his colleagues needed to decide their company's long-term use of the Internet in their business plan. It was a complicated and thorny issue. Should they get a Web site up fast and try to beat their competition or should they take it slow, figure out exactly what they wanted to offer online, and be more intentional about their approach?

Because his firm had been the industry leader, Steve felt it was more important to do it right rather than do it fast. He convinced his management to take their time and proceed in a studied and rational manner. But no more than two weeks later the competition launched one of the most impressive Internet sites around with services far beyond what his firm currently offered. "Here we were just trying to find a time to clear our calendars and meet to discuss the Internet. In the time it took us to scramble and get an online presence, our competitor started to erode our business. By waiting I had made a big mistake."

Steve likes to tell this story to the folks that work with him. It was a decision that he wasn't proud of but one he learned from. He encourages others to share their mistakes because it's in the failures that the lessons lurk. "Now I act with urgency on the things that truly deserve to be urgent."

Can you risk too often? Sure. Can there be too many failures? Absolutely. The wisdom of Fools is that they know when to use these skills. They do not overuse them. They are not predictable. They choose when and where to use the skills and artfully pick the right battles. The Fools' skills are tools in a toolbox. As Lao-Tzu says, "People usually fail when they are on the verge of success." The Fool can sense and almost predict when the success will occur. And if by chance it doesn't, the Fool knows when to let it go. Just as scientists redeem their accidents and make a breakthrough, so we can redeem our mistakes as well.

In 1985, Coke responded to the cola wars with Pepsi by introducing the biggest mistake of their history—New Coke. New Coke was a Pepsi copycat—a sweeter, less carbonated version of the original Coke formula. New Coke was met with a wash of confusion. What is the traditional Coke? Old Coke? How is New Coke different from Pepsi? Why would I want to buy it?

Coke found a failure in New Coke. Coca-Cola management pulled the plug and canceled New Coke. But they learned a lesson, one that has shaped the direction of the company's future. Leadership brands have intrinsic value. The Coca-Cola name is powerful. Ultimately Coke should be more concerned with its own road than bowing to the antics of the competition. The New Coke ordeal sharpened the senses of the company and gave them new momentum to act like a leader.

The Fool helps us honor the value of mistakes. Fools in business bring reverence to the point of weakness. They celebrate weakness by finding something instructive. They will not avoid mistakes but tend to look at them straight on. They study them with anticipation and hope.

When Avis entered the rental car market it was a distant competitor. Then they launched the "We Try Harder" campaign. Avis positioned themselves as a strong second-tier player and gained considerable market share. The vulnerability of being at the end of a long list of small companies was a vulnerability that they turned into a strength by becoming a strong second.

For the Fool, weakness reflects the underside of opportunity. The weakness is considered sacred.

Celebrate weakness by trying these exercises:

1. Become a student of vulnerability.

When tackling a challenge, consider the weaknesses present. What's the heart of the problem? What's the center of the dysfunction? Is there a soft underbelly here? What is the weakness that you or the corporation is trying to cover up? How can you make this weakness a strength?

2. Think of a failure you've had at work.

If you can't come up with one in one minute or less, then you are probably not taking enough risks. Practice being more bold. What are you passionate about? Stick with it.

Here is a summary of the key business principles of the Fool:

1. Run the other way: Invert conventional wisdom.
2. Reach over the top: Explore absurd solutions.
3. Persevere, persevere, and persevere again: Don't give up too soon.
4. Celebrate failure and find success: Explore weakness and redeem failure.

Fools and Teams

No doubt you've been in a group that has run out of ideas. The team is exhausted. You feel flat. You just haven't gotten it yet. If you invite in a Fool, he will show you the other side of the limitations, get you unstuck and on your way.

Fools are good roadblock busters. When a team has reached an impasse, when there are no good ideas at the end of the tunnel, Fools bust through and find new ways to approach the problem. Their ideas are often remarkable and they have many of them.

Fools will rise in responsibility from the sheer greatness of their ideas. It is, however, often hard to corral their talent within teams. Fools have a hard time compromising their vision. Corporate bodies of any description require compromise, yet the Fool isn't usually willing to do much of it. Fools enjoy collaborating with one or two creative partners and usually no more.

I have colleague who employs a very talented art director. The company cherishes his contributions. The irony is his manager expects that every three months the art director will quit. My colleague anticipates it; she knows this art director gets frustrated by the corporate process. Luckily she always finds new ways to encourage the art director to stay.

Because Fools are highly valuable to the organization. And yet Fools can be rare. There are usually no more than one or two in a business team.

Like the canaries coal miners took into the mines to sense when oxygen levels were low, Fools have a radar for when the corporate environment is becoming stifling to creativity. They are so sensitive to the truth, they are the first to know if there is enough creative fuel to run the engine. They will signal to others if there is reason for innovation distress.

Yet in a buisness renaissance, Fools are exactly what the firm needs to continually reinvent themselves. *Every team needs a Fool.* This makes it important to find ways to preserve the commitment of the Fools on your team—to keep them engaged in the work. It's up to the team and its leadership to find ways to keep them happy. More than other Faces of Genius, they need to be "handled with care." Because Fools are so important to the creative health of your organization, I'm going to give you more suggestions for keeping Fools around.

1. Let them know how much you need them.

Fools like to be acknowledged for their creative brain trust. We all do, but because Fools don't always feel "organization friendly," they need to be stroked and want validation for their ideas more than any other Face. Remember: Fools take pride in being Fools.

2. Give them as much autonomy as possible.

The best way to work with Fools is to give them free rein. They do best with lots of autonomy. Don't bog them down with too much process, or they will recoil. Let them have a forum where they can share their ideas.

3. Give them access to the highest levels of decision making possible.

Fools' ideas break boundaries and barriers. They need to be in a team with those who can find ways to negotiate the barriers and get their ideas implemented. Get them to the people who can get things done.

4. Try to find "partners" for Fools.

Fools need a partner to help them bust down the barriers. They need a colleague—usually a Sage—to round out the rough edges of the ideas and help them sell their concepts through an organization. They should be partnered with someone who is more open to compromise.

You'll find Fools in any field, but they tend to land in spots where they can influence change. They like to be where they can make lots of contributions. Fools find an ally and then stay in the political shadow. Once they have found a role for themselves where they can be free to create and fail, they stay there and make it home.

Pitfalls to Avoid

Fools pride themselves on being truth tellers, but Fools have some weaknesses to consider. The first is that Fools can forget that the truth almost always hurts. Fools are often unaware of how much foment their ideas cause for the team and the organization. They have a hard time understanding how much change needs to take place to implement their ideas and how painful the change is for others. Fools do well to be sensitive to the dynamics around them. While "genius disturbs and intrudes" as Jung said, it is still prudent to be as aware and compassionate as possible.

Fools also need to practice a measure of patience. While their perseverance can work in their favor, it can also turn ears deaf. Sometimes others begin to disregard Fools' input if they push without wisdom. Fools need to achieve a balance between knowing when to push and knowing when to back off. If Fools can use their perseverance as a way to provide creative growth for the organization, they will find satisfaction and offer valuable ideas.

The Five Faces of Genius Summary

	THE SEER	THE OBSERVER	THE ALCHEMIST	THE FOOL	THE SAGE
The Creative Power Principle	The Power to Image	The Power to Notice Detail	The Power to Connect Domains	The Power to Celebrate Weakness	The Power to Simplify
Key Creative Skill	Visualization	Ideas from the collection of detail Curiosity	Ideas from connection	Inversion Absurdity Perseverance	
Easy Way to Remember the Face	See it	Notice it	Mix it	Celebrate it	
Benefit to Teams	Vision for future Test possible outcomes	Conceptual thinking rooted in real issues	Insights through analogies	Ideas that break through barriers	
Pitfalls	Needs to combine Seer with other Faces	Can draw the wrong inferences from the detail	Can rely too heavily on others for idea stimulus	Can persevere beyond what's reasonable	

Exercises

You'll find the Fool skills easily added to your toolbox, but to master them requires focus. Try practicing again and again. Here are the first steps to begin.

1. List three weaknesses of your business as you see it:

1)

2)

3)

Try to turn the business weaknesses upside down. How might the weaknesses become strengths or be perceived to be strengths? Don't worry if the ideas seem absurd. What do you discover?

1)

2)

3)

2. Fools find unusual ways to surprise and delight. Think of the way Nordstrom lavishly takes care of its customers. Customers never have to leave the store for entertainment, refreshment, or even rest. If you treated your customers foolishly, what would you do?

1)

2)

3)

WORK DIFFERENTLY

Breaks Barriers with the Fool

Somewhere we learn creativity means freedom and the absence of limitations. We feel we need a blank canvas, no boundaries, no critiques to be a genuinely creative person. And that's why we think art and business are so different. There are no boundaries in art. The artist is free. Yet business is defined by boundaries. The manager is limited—by the organization, by the competition, by the market.

Fools, however, appreciate the barriers and celebrate them. For them, the limitations are the passageways to the breakthroughs. Once Fools know the limitations, then they can work at innovation. They learn the wisdom of limits.

1. Make friends with the limitations.

The great movie director Sidney Lumet described a conversation with another director, Akira Kurosawa. Lumet praised Kurosawa for the entry scene in the movie *Ran*. Lumet asked him how he set up such a tremendous shot for the epic film. Kurosawa described the creative process for the scene, which he shot at the Sony movie studio. He said he couldn't pan to the left because the camera would catch the Sony factory building. If he panned to the right, then he would catch the airport runway. He was limited. So he shot the set dead on. The restrictions made the scene stunning.

Sometimes we feel the limitations are enemies. But we can often invent by finding a way to embrace the limitations.

A business artist needed to launch a product with what she considered to be a small budget. She felt restricted. The product needed to perform well. There were lots of expectations, but little money. She wondered what inventive ideas she could develop that would stretch her resources. How could she make friends with her limitations? She designed what she called an OPM strategy—Other Peoples' Money. She solicited three strategic partners who went into a joint venture and made it possible for her to launch the product the way she had intended to do it. What we lack or are denied within our work can become the ground for fertile ideas.

2. Intensify the limitations.

My husband and I were recently in Napa, California, and toured a winery. We learned some of the very best wines—wines with the most complex tastes—come from vines that are stressed. The wine master purposely stresses the vine—denies it water, nutrient-rich soil, and shade, all to produce the most exquisite grapes. Sometimes it is the stress of our restrictions that can provide the best results.

Instead of trying to topple the barriers, invert your approach. Try enhancing the barriers, making them even more restrictive, and see what you find as a creative result.

The biggest threat to Crayola's business has been the entry of computer games for kids. Instead of drawing and coloring, kids are tempted by interactive CDs and more. Instead of trying to dominate computer games, Crayola has chosen to flourish within their limitations. They do children's art products better than anyone, and have expanded their market to include markers and innovative drawing tools. They honored the barriers and found a deeper path.

3. Let the limitations instruct you, not bind you.

When I was in the advertising industry, I complained that client assignments felt like doing aerobics in a closet. When asked to create a campaign, the client wanted great work, but the parameters were so well defined it seemed impossible to create. The ad had to say x, couldn't say y, couldn't imply z. Legal had to review it. Public relations had to review it. Clients had to run it by their mother-in-law. With every inventive move, we would hit the limitation of the floor, the walls, or the ceiling of the closet.

The funny thing, though, was we almost always came up with big ideas, in spite of the limitations. Even in the presence of barriers, we had breakthrough ideas. In fact, over time we developed wisdom about the barriers. We figured out what limitations were solid and couldn't be compromised and which were porous and could be pushed. They instructed us.

Psychologist Rollo May tells us that when we hear there are "unlimited possibilities" or "all options are open," it is a defeating message. When we don't have limitations, we become discouraged and deflated. There are too many options to consider.

It's the same in business. *It is not the absence of limitations that makes for creativity, but understanding the nature of the limitations.* The wisdom of the Fool teaches us to know how to understand the landscape of the boundaries, what they are, and how much power each holds.

Respecting the Via Negativa at Work

The Fool agrees with the theologian Matthew Fox's definition of creativity as a dialogue between the Via Positiva and the Via Negativa. The Via Positiva is the time when ideas flow, when ideas are abounding. You feel idea fertile. Life is good. Directly translated, it is the Positive Way.

The Via Negativa is the Negative Way. These are the downtimes, the dry spells, the creative blocks. You have to work for an idea. It's painful. The Via Negativa is the shadow side of our creative process. It's the side we hide from others and from ourselves.

In the workplace, Via Positiva is cherished and even worshipped. When you've got great ideas you're hot. Others see how valuable you are. You are a rising star. But the Via Negativa is anathema. If you're not delivering ideas, folks think you are dried up. You think you are dried up. Your imagination spirals down. You lose confidence in your genius.

But Fools respect the Via Negativa. They know invention requires a back-and-forth rhythm between the Via Positiva and the Via Negativa. The Negative Way is an essential part of your creative spirit. To have fertile times you have to have fallow times—even in business. The Via Negativa is natural and valuable.

Here's how the Fool helps you care for your creative spirit when the Via Negativa comes.

1. Give up.

Philosopher William James said that we learn to swim in the winter and skate in the summer. When we abandon our focus and give up the search for ideas for a season, then we find our solutions. A season can be an hour, a day, or a week. Give up on the problem for a while. When you rest for a while, ideas trickle upward from your unconscious mind. Let your mind lie fallow.

2. Doubt yourself.

You don't always have to feel creative to be a creative person. All creativity works in concert with doubt. Doubt is the signal you are risking. The premier signal of the creative life.

While Cézanne was revolutionizing the art world with his painting, he was filled with doubt about his work. Accept doubt as your "idea partner."

3. Avoid self-critique.

Richard Feynman wrote, "I've very often made mistakes in my physics by thinking the theory isn't as good as it really is, thinking that there are lots of complications that are going to spoil it."

Don't overcritique your work. Sometimes the self-examination is harder than any other outside source you'll encounter.

4. Memorize the problem and do something else.

Le Corbusier, the great Bauhaus architect, would memorize the parameters of a new assignment and then wait three months before tackling the design. During that interval, new ideas would be growing in his mind. You and I would call this scheduling innovation time— giving time for his muse to speak.

Now, few corporations give the luxury of three months to cogitate, but the discipline of memorizing the problem and then waiting for a while before designing a solution is a good one. Build time for dreaming into a project schedule.

5. Practice dreamy dozing.

George Eliot said, "One morning as I was lying in bed, thinking what should be the subject of my first story, my thoughts merged themselves into a dreamy doze, and I imagined myself writing a story of which the title was 'The Sad Fortunes of the Reverend Amos Barton.' And so this became the title of her first successful novel.

The Via Negative respects the time when you are only partially conscious of the problem. Be sure to take minibreaks that allow for transitions from focused work to relaxation.

6. Question like a scientist

The Nobel Prize–winning physicist I. I. Rabi says he became a scientist because of his mother. When Rabi came home from school, his mother didn't ask him, "What did you learn today?" She asked him, "What questions did you ask today?"

Sometimes we get stuck because we have too tightly defined the boundaries. Even when you believe you've asked the right questions of the business, keep on asking. The questions dislodge creative blocks. The questions keep the dialogue going with the Via Negativa. The Negative Way always has something to say.

5. THE SAGE

THE POWER TO SIMPLIFY

"The art of art, the glory of expression, the sunshine of the light of letters, is simplicity."
—WALT WHITMAN

Anita Roddick, founder of The Body Shop, said, "The idea for the shop was so simple, it hardly merits being described as an 'idea' at all." In the United Kingdom, hand lotion and body creams were sold in big containers. Roddick felt this was inconvenient and didn't want to buy more lotion than she needed. With the creation of The Body Shop, Roddick simply offered a retail "beauty bar" in which customers could buy a small jar of lotion and refill it for a charge. A simple inspiration. It was a business breakthrough generated by the power of simplification.

The final Face of Genius is the Sage. In this chapter we'll work to integrate this two-pronged approach of the Sage:

1. Sages use simplicity as the path to ideas.
2. Sages access history as the ground for inspiration.

By learning these final Sage principles, you will fully round out your creative style and master all Five Faces of Genius.

The Creative Genius of the Sage: To Imagine More, Imagine Less

When Martha Graham began dancing in the early 1900s, the high art of dance was considered to be the Russian ballet. Ballet with its refined movement, exquisite costuming, and adorned set and stage. The ballet was the pinnacle of the discipline.

Graham thought differently. She believed dance was a visceral thing, that it should be about the body, not about the ornamentation of the body. She said, "Movement never lies." For Graham, the purpose of dance was the celebration of the human spirit through movement.

So Graham stripped the complexity of ballet to its essence—human movement. Instead of predictable dance steps, she used the motion of the entire body. Instead of ornate sets, her stage was clear. Instead of elaborate costuming, she wore simple clothes. In the piece titled "Lamentation," she danced wearing a long tube of jersey fabric. She wanted the audience to interpret her message through the movement of her body.

This is how she described the simplicity of her work: "When a dancer is at the peak of his power, he has two lovely, fragile, and perishable things. One is the spontaneity that is arrived at over years of training. The other is simplicity, but not the usual kind. It is the state of complete simplicity costing no less than absolutely everything, of which T. S. Eliot speaks."

Graham's groundbreaking contributions changed the discipline of dance forever. Using the principles of the Sage, she became an originator of modern dance and created a signature style that continues to this day.

FOR THE SAGE, SIMPLICITY IS THE PATH TO IDEAS

Simplicity that costs no less than everything constitutes the creative genius of the Sage. The act of creation occurs when an idea is stripped to its essence through the taking away of what is superficial and by getting to the core. The photographer Alfred Stieglitz described the artistic demand as "to exclude everything that is unessential to a clear statement of the dominant underlying idea." This is the powerful message the Sage brings to our creative soul: that by cherishing the essential, you can navigate great mystery and find innovative power.

The writer Ernest Hemingway excluded the unessential and showed this genius of the Sage. His masterpieces *A Farewell to Arms* and *For Whom the Bell Tolls* defined a breakthrough literary style called journalistic. Short, terse sentences with little description. He used a bare-bones English that communicated a world with an economy of words. In eliminating explanation he would breed his art. It is said Hemingway did more to change the style of prose than any other writer in the twentieth century. Hemingway's genius was his ability to tell the story simply and yet profoundly. Sages have an inherent wisdom that informs their creative energy. They know what is simple is elegant.

I traveled to the Museum of Contemporary Art in Chicago and was captivated by the mobiles of Alexander Calder. Some are small. Others are grand and fill a room. But you are overcome by the power of their simplicity. Standing under his structures, you realize he was a master of reduction who made mobiles into an art form.

One of his mobiles is called *Fish*. He showed the bones, the scales, and gave an inkling of what he wanted you to see. He reduced objects to their central essence and communicated them with power and grace. Like an archaeologist, he digs through the unessential, comes up with the core, and shows you the essence of his art.

In an age when we have access to unlimited information, the skills of the Sage help us focus on how to generate a new idea without getting caught in the trap of searching endlessly for more. When you use the Sage skill of homing in on the essentials, you can peel away all that is distracting and find an inspiration at the center. You imagine more by imagining less.

Many scientists and mathematicians call simplicity the evidence of true invention. When theories or calculations are elegant, there is a refreshed power and conviction in their truth. The experimenter knows that when simplicity takes over, one has wrested something from the gods. Have you ever had that sense? The idea that was so simple, it almost startles you? Some talk about it as if the answer had been in front of them all along and they just stumbled on it. When you find that simple solution, you know you have found the genius of the Sage within.

The simplicity of the Sage is sometimes compared to falling in love. Someone may be working on the "problem" of finding a partner, but as they date they can't seem to find their soulmate. Something surprising happens when they begin to see an old friend in a new light, someone they never would have considered as a love interest. They realize over time they've fallen in love with a friend. They found the simple solution that was in front of them all along.

We talked earlier about Andrew Wiles's mathematical breakthrough solving Fermat's last theorem. This is how he expressed the genius moment, "So indescribably beautiful, it was so simple and so elegant . . . and I just stared in disbelief." When we've found the simple idea, we've found the Sage. It's this simplicity that demands no less than everything we can cultivate in our own creative spirit.

SAGES VALUE HISTORY AS THE INSPIRATION FOR IDEAS

While mastering the art of simplicity, the Sage also creates by accessing wisdom from the past. Sages have a recollective ability that allows them to capture ideas from the past and recast them for the present. In so doing they create something with new merit today.

Think of the Sage as an ancient wise one—a buddha perhaps—who has deep wisdom to share. Someone who clears away the confusion and then smacks you with the obvious wisdom you didn't think to consider. One who knows both the simple truth of the present and the wisdom of the past.

Martha Graham describes this second aspect of the Sage best. She believed fragments of memories from the past inform our present creations; that those who have gone before us shape the inspiration of the present. So when speaking of genius, Graham said that a better expression describing the act of creation would be "a retriever, a lovely strong golden retriever that brings things back from the past, or retrieves things from our common blood memory." It is the wisdom from the past that inspires our creativity today.

When we think of our personal history, our heritage, or our creativity, we find ideas that prod us toward invention. Sages are similar to Alchemists in that they draw their inspiration from an analogy, but what makes Sages unique is that they find their idea from what has gone before. You can see this at work in the genius of a writer or director who tells an old story and makes it fresh for today. The movie *East of Eden* was a remake of the Cain and Abel story from the Old Testament. The animated Disney movie *Anastasia* rekindled the original film version with Yul Brynner and Ingrid

Bergman. The Sage taps the spirit of generations past, rekindles old break-throughs, and reapplies them to the present in some unique way.

Think of the creative power of Martin Luther King Jr. His influence on American culture was a mark of genius in the twentieth century. The march he led on Washington was one of the largest public demonstrations in American history: 250,000 people gathered to protest racial segregation. Where did he find the inspiration for this philosophy of nonviolence? One inspiration was King's studies of Mahatma Gandhi—from the wisdom of the past. Gandhi believed that the most effective and lasting change for the disenfranchised was through nonviolent means. King recognized the strug-gle of American blacks and saw the similarities to the Indian divisions. He reapplied the wisdom of the past to the present to create one of the most important breakthroughs in race relations history.

Sages are history addicts. History is like a manual that offers them a guide for living in the present. So it follows that Sages love stories. They believe in the transforming power of a narrative—that when we hear story, we are touched like no other form of communication. By remembering and telling stories, Sages change today with eternal truths from the past.

The genius of a great movie lies in this power to tell a story. Think of the greatest movies you've seen. *Gone With the Wind. Star Wars. To Kill a Mockingbird.* These stories stay with us. We reflect on them. They help us mark times in our lives. Our stories are a heritage and stimulus for great ideas. Who captivates you with the power of their stories? A grandparent? Friend? Colleague? They have the power to hold your attention and make you listen. It's as if you are spellbound and can't pull yourself away from the tale. When you master the Sage, you learn the ancient power of story and put it to work in your creative life.

The ideas of the Sage have a timeless quality. It's as if the thought is as strong today as it ever was. That's why art in museums continues to inspire us. It represents a strata of human understanding that exists above everyday life. That is also why we have a "Classics" category in bookstores. The sto-ries still hold us. They are about the deepest writhings and joys of the human spirit. They are timeless.

So the Sage can lead us through the journey of our imagination. Let the Sage take you by the hand. Shed all you do not need and find the wis-dom that has gone before.

Mastering the Sage at Work

When you consider the genius of Nordstrom, you think of service. They employ salespeople who care, service professionals who will go the extra mile. They pride themselves on personal and friendly service. Nordstrom has a very simple policy for hiring people who will succeed in their environment: Hire nice people. That's it. Hire nice people. The theory is that it's almost impossible to train a not-nice person to become a nice person. Hire nice people—a simple human relations policy that is the lynchpin to a Nordstrom successful business strategy.

Here are the Sage skills that you can put to work on your business today. The Sage brings both simplicity and the power of history to the practice of business artistry. Let's look at how to master both.

FOCUS ON THE HIGH, HOLY CALLING

Sages know where they are going. They define what they believe their company should be about and then focus all they do to make sure that happens. Sages follow their purpose at work with a singular focus.

Listen to this business artist, Jackson. "I have recently taken on a new role in the last few months. The part of the organization that I manage was in considerable turmoil, having lacked consistent leadership and direction. Everyone was trying to do the right thing, but nobody was doing the *same* thing. As I entered the picture I modified the internal structure a bit, identified a manageable number of tasks, put them in priority order, and articulated my definition of success for each. I reminded the team of what the purpose of this company is and how their roles helped us get there. By 'uncomplicating' the task list and giving each a priority, we've been able to do more . . . and more successfully."

Don't you wish you had a manager like Jackson? He focused the team on the highest calling. He eliminated what was unessential and redefined the core issues. His breakthrough leadership ideas were generated by his Sage style. He simplified the process, marshaled the group, and helped them use their gifts together.

Sages regularly assess how their personal actions align with where the firm is going. They discard tasks that do not support the long-term vision of the company. Not only do Sages focus on core issues, they relish core issues. They get a high from concentrating on what really matters within their work and from helping others stay focused on the high, holy calling.

Biogen is one of the world's leading biotech companies. Developing new products in the drug industry is a time-consuming and expensive process. Years go into the research, clinical trials, and FDA approval. James Tobin took over the leadership of Biogen in the early 1990s when the company was developing two potentially successful drugs—Avonex, for multiple sclerosis patients; and Hirulog, a therapy for heart disease patients.

Tobin had been CEO for just a few months when the clinical trials proved Hirulog was not much more effective against heart disease than a competitive product on the market. Tobin faced the challenge of focusing the resources of the company to ensure long-term profitability. But could he split the company's energy between the two drugs? Could the firm afford to drop either? What was the highest calling of the company?

Tobin decided to concentrate on Avonex rather than Hirulog. He said, "Let's devote all of our resources to getting one thing right." As a consequence, the entire organization shifted its focus and prepared Avonex for market, and the product successfully launched in 1996. Tobin used the skills of the Sage to pursue one product rather than two. Simplifying forces led to a breakthrough.

Using the Sage tools can become second nature. Focusing on the high, holy calling is a discipline you administer to yourself just like working out at the gym or taking vitamins. Every time you face opportunity, grill yourself about the purpose behind what you are doing. It will keep you honest. It will also guide you to leadership ideas.

I love the Sage story of Andy Grove at Intel. For years Intel's primary business had been memory chips. But as the industry changed, Grove believed the company needed to change. Microprocessors were the technology on the rise, and Grove thought the company should shift gears and focus on microprocessors. Grove took the lead and made the decision to simplify the product line to microprocessors alone. Grove's change to microprocessors is widely recognized as the decision that made Intel the industry leader. From the time Grove took over Intel in 1987 until he left in 1998, revenues grew eight fold. Using the skills of the Sage, Grove focused the organization and found a stroke of business genius.

Job one for someone interested in improving their Sage skills is to practice being ruthless. Ask yourself, "What is the heart of this issue? What's the high, holy calling?" See if you can peel away the layers and get to the hard core. What is it? Once you've done this, you'll find new ideas will rise to the surface.

If the Sage skills are an opportunity area for you, start here:

1. State your high, holy calling at work.

What do you want to get from this time in your career? What do you want to give to your firm? Define the highest best for you where you are at work today.

2. Practice distilling ideas to the essence.

When someone shares an idea, or when you generate one yourself, try to make it more simple. If you take away what is extraneous to an idea, you often find the heart of what makes it magical. Sages deconstruct, they disassemble, they divine what is essential and unessential within an idea. By coalescing the complex, they find insight.

FIND THE STRAIGHTEST STREET TO MARKET

Sages can simplify systems and find new ways to go to market. They drill through the unessential and find new roads to sell products, services, ideas. The genius of Michael Dell was his ability to simplify the complexity of manufacturing and the selling of computers. Dell believed selling computers was just too difficult. To be a successful retailer, you had to carry the right product and the right amount of product. To be a successful manufacturer, you had to sell through distributors and retailers that siphoned away profits. For Michael Dell the difficulty was a signal. Complexity is a sign to a Sage that opportunity lurks in the tangled bushes. Like a vulture circling prey, Sages can sense when great ideas are near just by paying attention to the presence of complexity.

Dell created a process in which computers are custom made for clients. Dell works directly with individuals and companies to design PCs for their needs. Customers don't have to bother going to a retail shop or working with a distributor. They buy direct. They can even call for toll-free tech support and next-day, on-site service.

Now Dell allows customers to buy direct over the Internet. Dell can take an order for a computer and deliver it within twenty-four hours. Michael Dell says, "We're always looking to see what we can do to make our customers' lives easier or save them money." By directly meeting the needs of their customers, Dell's stock gained 87,000 percent from 1990 to 1999. It is a $12 billion business created by using the skills of the Sage. Dell took what was previously a complicated process, simplified it, and created breakthrough. He imagined more by imagining less.

Become a lookout scout for complexity and confusion. When you sense it on the horizon, you are close to opportunity. When you finally see the contour of the complex business problem—whether it's the way you work with other departments, the way your services are priced, or the way you communicate with your boss—then you can begin to use the Sage skills. Start to simplify. Notice what is unessential. What is at the heart of what's going on? How can you straighten the street and create new opportunity?

In the mid-1990s Procter & Gamble faced the challenge of growing their huge portfolio of brands in a stagnating market. One of the ways they had grown in the past was to create line extensions. Take Crest, for example. There was Tartar Control Crest, Sparkle Crest, Cool Mint Crest, Advanced Formula Crest. The list went on and on, fifty-two versions in all. And this proliferation wasn't just exemplified by Crest. It plagued many of their other brands as well.

Procter & Gamble realized that they were confusing their own consumers. Folks had to stand in front of the shelves and stare for minutes to decide what to buy. In an effort to meet every little need, they had befuddled their own consumer.

P&G made a Sage move. They simplified things. They sifted through the brands and eliminated products that weren't selling as well. They cut the number of Head & Shoulders shampoo items from thirty-one to fifteen. Some were worried their sales would go down. That was the surprise. Their market share increased! They cut the complexity and trimmed the line to their own advantage. They picked the straightest road to market.

But getting straight to market can mean commonplace ideas as well. Imagine a Sage behind the counter at an espresso bar. A Sage would figure out the simplest way to handle the drink order. He would set up the beans, the milk, the flavorings, the cups and tops in the manner that would make for the most efficient work possible. When you master the Sage you ask yourself, "Where am I going and how can I get there simply?"

"Getting work through the bank was a nightmare." These are the words of a loan officer at a large national bank. Celeste knew processing loans took forever in their organization. It seemed everyone had to touch it, add to it, quality control it. Celeste said, "I knew that to become nimble, it had to stop." She pondered how to simplify and bring wisdom to the process. "I designed a workflow process that meant loans could be processed internally in twenty-four hours. I reconfigured the procedures and the approval process. I used my Sage tools and saved the company time and saved my sanity!" It was as if Celeste untangled a single thread and shortened the path for her firm to be more competitive in the market.

To improve your Sage skills, stop obsessing about your ideas. Henry James said that ideas that were overworked "smelled like too much lamp." When we burn too much oil, we try too hard. We mistakenly believe a more sophisticated answer is demanded of us.

But it is often the simple solution, even the obvious one, that leads to innovation. It's as if something great is at our feet and we are still looking out over the horizon. Ask yourself what solutions are close enough to "stumble" on.

Notice elegance in your work. As we said, scientists often call equations ugly if they are too complicated. Good ideas in any field are elegant. There is a sense of fitness to the ideas, a craftsmanship.

Begin to notice what is elegant:

1. Sages write the last sentence first.

Think about what you finally want to say or what you finally want to have happen before you begin a project. How do you want this conversation to end? What outcome do you want from this meeting? When you "write the last sentence first" it will help you determine where you want to go and the straightest street will be easy to find.

2. Imagine you are the complexity police.

What are the places in your work process where things are tangled? How can you straighten it out?

TO LOOK FORWARD, LOOK BACK

Now let's turn to the second principle of the creativity of the Sage. Earlier I said one of the gifts of the Sage is the ability to look to history. Business artists find nuggets of inspiration that have been passed down and rekindled for the present. When you incorporate the skills of the Sage, you can take insights from the past and find how they might be reborn today.

Nathan Myhrvold, a former Microsoft technical guru, said it best: "Every day I have to make difficult decisions and I base them primarily on what has happened in the past. History can lead you to see important abstractions, and it also offers great lessons in the need to avoid wild and tempting speculations about the future." By surveying and understanding the past, you can transform and re-create the present.

Managers often make the mistake that we have to create something that feels entirely new to break through. We can't forget that the past, while radically different in some ways, can have important similarities with the present; that rescuing nuggets from the past can be a way to break through the limitations of today. Become a student of history.

Jane is an urban planner for a large architectural firm. Her company won the contract to design the town hall and marketplace for a small but growing city. Much of the growth of the city had come from technology firms locating in the area. Many of these folks worked from home. While telecommuting provided the chance to be with family, for many families in the small town, technology had isolated them. The city commissioners wanted to revitalize the urban center and make it a place for community and for gathering.

Jane was intrigued by the project but really stumped about how to pro-ceed. Rather than just impose her idea of what community gathering would be, she decided to look to history for some wisdom. She began to study the city centers of the ancient societies. What did they look like? How was commerce handled? Transportation? She learned from the Greeks how important the spiritual temples were for gathering; from the Chinese she gleaned the importance of the marketplace. In her design, she drew from the wisdom of the past to create common areas that were not just effi-cient but sensitive to humans. "I used my Sage skills by dipping into the past and making it come alive for today."

One of the clearest ways to see this sense of recollective history is to look to new products. The 1960s saw the creation of the Volkswagen Beetle. An inexpensive and simply adorable car, the Bug began a craze. When 1960s retro came to style in the late 1990s, Volkswagen reinvented the Bug and introduced it in 1998. It became an instant success. The Bug raised so much attention that folks were saying it wasn't a car for shy people. Strangers approached owners and asked to see the car up close. Celebrities like Cindy Crawford and Jerry Seinfeld were buying them right and left. Volkswagen took a good idea from the past and rekindled it for the present.

Here's another new product idea whose inspiration came from the past. A Spanish toy inventor was visiting a museum and noticed an ancient Greek game on exhibit. It featured the knuckle bones of sheep, which children used as a game. Kids painted pictures on the bones and then played a game with them similar to marbles.

The inventor had an idea. Perhaps this game could be reinvented for today. He created the toy craze called Crazy Bones. Crazy Bones are made with plastic and feature sixty different characters. Kids collect them, trade pieces, and have to replace them when they "lose" to friends. It's an idea built on the back of history and widely popular today.

Looking back is the key the Sage offers to opening the future. You can remember what has gone before and change what is to come. Look back to your own experience for ideas. Try to keep your past experience at the forefront. For Sages, getting to their past is as easy as accessing a database of lessons learned. They quickly translate them to present-day challenges.

A pharmaceutical salesperson, Robin, was asked to make a presentation to a group of colleagues on his recent success and how he was able to meet his goals on a particularly difficult product line. His first presentation was well prepared, a good PowerPoint show with lots of charts and graphs. But halfway into it, he realized he was boring the audience. Someone was nodding his head as if he were going to fall asleep. Robin said, "Clearly, I wasn't holding their attention. I had to think fast."

Robin asked himself a Sage question, "When in the past have I had to keep a group's attention?" He remembered the story he had told to his child's kindergarten class a few years back about his travels to Africa. The story captivated the kids. Could he tell a story about selling this new drug and wake up the audience? When Robin found a place to stop, he paused, turned off the computer, walked out from behind the podium, and said, "Now that you have the background, let me tell you a story." He immediately got the crowd's attention. He launched into the story of his first sale of the pharmaceutical product—how he persisted in getting the meeting; how nervous he was; how surprised he was when the doctor agreed to try it. He told it with all the excitement of a fairy tale. When he finished, the group was captivated. The kindergarten experience gave Robin the idea he needed to rescue himself.

Clients who score high in Sage skills say their first creative step is to search their past to locate when they have encountered similar problems. In another job? At another client? With another customer? A Sage once said to me, "The first thing I do when I begin searching for ideas is to figure out where I have encountered this type of problem before. It's my first instinct." The Sage uses the experience as a springboard for discovering some new idea.

Those who struggle with the Sage often find it hard to appreciate the past. So to enhance your Sage skills, begin to look back:

1. Make a mental scrapbook about the past ideas you've contributed at work.

Write these ideas in a business journal. This can be the start of looking back for creative inspiration. To look forward, look back.

2. Identify a problem that hounds you in your work, then think of someone from your past with wisdom.

If he were to give you pearls of advice, what would he tell you to do?

LET A STORY LOOSE

I picked up a Patagonia catalog and read a story about one of the first products the company ever created. It was a pair of knickers with a wide wale corduroy that could only be woven at one loom in Lancashire. It was such a challenging process and quality was so important to them that Patagonia had to bring old weavers out of retirement to operate the ancient loom.

Business artists are enthralled by the transforming power of stories. When a story is told, Sages believe it can create a new understanding of the company and a new commitment to it. When the stories are passed from employee to employee, they inspire and even create a culture of change. Of risk taking. Of rule breaking.

You can inspire folks around you by collecting and telling stories. The

Sage tells these stories to others within the corporation. They can be large ideas like the Patagonia story or even small ones about colleagues you know who broke through the status quo and brought ideas to work.

At Polaroid everyone knows the story about the creation of the Land camera. It is a constant reminder that innovation is a core part of the company's philosophy. "At Polaroid we have a story about the beginning of instant photography. Land was taking pictures of his little daughter, Jennifer, and after a while she looked up at him and said, 'Daddy, why can't I see the pictures right away?' And bingo, that was the beginning of the idea. This question and insight led to Land's creating the outlines for the whole instant photographic system in a matter of a couple of days." This story encourages employees to pursue creative ideas. When you proclaim someone has created, it instills the belief that it can happen again. Stories change people.

I have a client who creates change by operating as the corporate memory of the company. Marilyn has been with the company for ten years. When someone asks her about the firm's past, she can tell legends about ideas, people, products, and enumerate their success and foibles. She is a walking search engine. You can ask her dates, products, and themes, and she can pull up for you what the company did and when and where. But she does more than just remember it. These points fuel her creative fire. She uses these historical points as building blocks for new ideas. She also uses them to augment the ideas of others and help set their ideas in a historical context for the organization. During one workshop evening, a number of people clustered around Marilyn and listened to her tell the great corporate stories of the past. One person said, "I could have listened to her for hours." The corporate memory serves to entertain and instruct, but more important, to inspire. The insight of the past came to the present through the power of the stories.

Creative teams are led by those who remember the history of breakthroughs and are able to illustrate the similarities and differences between them. Sages polish the corporation's stories of invention.

So polish your stories. What are the ways you broke through and innovated? Your colleagues? Your firm? Once you have them polished, share them. You'll be surprised how your creative leadership is bolstered and recognized. Learn to listen for the stories and cherish them. They will guide you to ideas.

And remember, for Sages, theory is less valuable than the raw experience. They are less interested in analysis. They want to know the story of what happened. They get their inspiration from the narrative. The story has more texture. It gives them more contact highs for inspiration.

Amazon.com's hiring practices reflect this preference for experience rather than theory. When interviewing candidates, they pay little attention to job history or even to what candidates think they can contribute to the firm. Candidates are asked questions about their personal values and interests, and given real-time scenarios to consider. Mr. Risher, an Amazon.com executive, puts it this way: "I might ask, 'How would you design a car for a deaf person?' Some people freeze when they get a question like that . . . but the best candidates say they'd plug their ears and drive around in their cars to experience what it feels like to be a deaf driver." By proposing scenarios to solve, Mr. Risher gets an experience of the candidates' qualities, not just scripted theories of who they want to be. The real-time experience is more valuable than the theory.

So begin to wrap your mind around the two skills of the Sage—simplicity and accessing truths of history:

1. Polish a story about your firm.

If you were asked to tell a story of creative breakthrough at your firm, what would it be? Then polish that story and tell it to others. You'll generate a wider culture of positive energy and innovation.

2. Polish a story about yourself.

If you were asked to tell a story of a time you were creative at work, what would that story be? Then polish it and tell it to yourself often. Be prepared to share it with others. You'll find your reputation as an idea leader soar.

Here is a summary of the key business principles of the Sage:

1. Focus on the high, holy calling: Focus like a laser on core issues.
2. Find the straightest street to market: Strip away the unessentials.
3. To look forward, look back: Find insight from rekindling the past.
4. Let a story loose: Identify and spread stories of positive change.

Sages and Teams

In teams, Sages tend to be very clear in their direction. They are internally motivated. The Sages' sense of direction focuses the group. These are the folks who ask, "Why are we doing what we are doing?"

Sages are often the first to frame the issue. They will say, "This is what we need to accomplish" or, "This is the task at hand." A health-care services manager might start a meeting, "We need to come up with a way to deal with the dissatisfaction patients have with our services. The heart of the issue is this: we are serving too many people per clinic. How can we even out the number of patients that attend our clinics?"

A business artist describes his creative style as a Sage: "My team will be having a discussion and the conversation has drifted way out in the weeds. I'm the one who pulls us back, restates why we are here and what we are up to. The practice focuses the creative energy of the team." This clarity of purpose characterizes the Sage.

Sages have a keen eye for truth. Consider the manager who runs a finance team responsible for working with the operations group. The finance team complains about how much money the operations people spend and how few of them take their recommendations to heart. The finance team leader wonders aloud, "Maybe the miscommunication isn't with the operations team, but with us. How can we design our message of cost savings so they can hear it better? If we talked to them like a customer, not a co-worker, how would we approach them?" Like distilling impurities from water, this business artist distills the communication problem to its essence.

Sages like the leadership role in creative situations. However, they need to be cautious. As leaders, they may not allow for enough divergence of views. To keep things on-task, Sages can truncate discussion too early or unknowingly guide it down the path they prefer. A manager describes his struggle with a Sage leader: "He always opens up the discussion and asks for ideas. After a few minutes of sharing our thoughts, he uses the time as a forum to share his ideas and then we break with a plan to pursue his ideas. I sometimes feel he doesn't go wide enough with the possible solutions." The Sage has to be careful to avoid this early narrowing of ideas.

This narrowing happens because Sages like simple truths rather than complex meanings. For the Sage, complexity is a sign of forces contrary to creativity. The Sage wants something smooth and elegant, an idea that rolls off the tongue. If it isn't simple, it's suspect. This means that if an idea seems too complex, they will reject it or try to pare it down to its key elements.

Yet Sage principles are helpful for group discussion. Because there is a herd mentality in groups, the topic can easily drift from the central focus. The Sage ropes the group back to the core issue. I have a colleague who is a master at the Sage. His favorite expression is, "Let's cut to the chase." In effect, he leads the group back to the central purpose of the discussion.

Because Sages value corporate memory, they draw from the past of the company and use it as a starting point for team discussion. "How have we handled similar situations in the past? How did that solution work for us?"

Sages are found in all business disciplines but rise in general management because of their ability to make complex notions simple. They take a wide variety of information and coalesce it into something tangible.

A SAGE TEAM EXERCISE

Ask the group to identify the heart of the issue at hand. Each member should define what they believe to be the core problem. As you survey the team, the group will hear different slants and perspectives. Don't try to gain consensus, just express the essence in unique ways. Next, ask each person to develop solutions around the core issue as they've defined it. You'll see a broad range of ideas that will spark new breakthroughs.

Pitfalls to Avoid

Remember to use both aspects of the Sage. The Sage is about simplicity but also about accessing wisdom. The Sage finds threads from the past that can be woven into the present. Find the few eternal stories and reapply them for today.

A weaknesses the Sage needs to be aware of is the slant toward austerity. The Sage can sometimes neglect important information that can lead to great ideas. They can sacrifice too much that is valuable to a concept when they simplify. Don't be overwhelmed by complexity or nuance. Often these are clues to a creative concept.

Sages also have to avoid looking back too much. The Sage may believe that there are no new ideas and try to rehash the past. Others may perceive them as too backward focused.

The Five Faces of Genius Summary

	THE SEER	THE OBSERVER	THE ALCHEMIST	THE FOOL	THE SAGE
The Creative Power Principle	The Power to Image	The Power to Notice Detail	The Power to Connect Domains	The Power to Celebrate Weakness	The Power to Simplfy
Key Creative Skill	Visualization	Ideas from the collection of detail Curiosity	Ideas from connection	Inversion Absurdity Perseverance	Simplification Ideas from history and story
Easy Way to Remember the Face	See it	Notice it	Mix it	Celebrate it	Simplify it
Benefit to teams	Vision for future Test possible outcomes	Conceptual thinking rooted in real issues	Insights through analogies	Ideas that break through barriers	Insight to key issues
Pitfalls	Needs to combine Seer with other Faces	Can draw the wrong inferences from the detail	Can rely too heavily on others for idea stimulus	Can persevere beyond what's reasonable	Can eliminate the messy margins that spawn good ideas

Exercises

When you've added the Sage to your toolbox of creative principles, you'll see how your idea leadership will unfold. Begin with these exercises and use the disciplines here frequently. They are questions you can ask again and again.

1. What seems to be the most complex issue on the business right now? Describe it briefly here.

_____

_____

_____

Create two simple solutions:

_____

_____

Create two more:

_____

_____

2. What wisdom from the business in the past could be relevant for today?

_____

_____

_____

WORK DIFFERENTLY

How the Sage Helps You Succeed in the Idea Economy

How often have you heard the expression, "I'm overloaded" or, "I'm doing the work of three people" or, "I had fifty voice mail messages last night." I once asked a colleague in the elevator how she was doing and she frantically replied, "I'm crazed!"

Listen to the subtext of these comments. "I'm doing the work of three people, because I'm so capable and I'm the only one that can handle it." "I got fifty voice mail messages because I'm so valuable and everyone needs to talk to me." "I'm crazed because I'm so critical to the success of this firm."

At some level, we choose this imbalance of administration winning out over implementation. We simply allow ourselves to take it on. We feel our jobs are more secure if we are overly busy. But as a business artist once told me, "I worry that the folks who stay here all night and work are weird. They need to be at the office working instead of someplace else for a reason. And it isn't because there is too much do. It's because they have *nothing else* to do."

The Sage skills help us focus on the high, holy calling—what really matters. In an idea economy, what matters is your ideas and making more ideas. The Sage strips away what is not essential—the administrative opium—and helps us work on the business of ideas.

Here are some suggestions for working more productively in the economy of ideas.

1. Don't just take projects, make projects.

Regularly assess the types of projects you are working on. What specifically are you learning? Write it down in your business journal. Record it and catalog it. Begin to look for patterns in what you are learning. What expertise are you developing? If your learning has diminished or stopped, then begin to wonder why and remedy it.

Sometimes remedying it means looking for a new position in your firm or a new position in a new company. *More often it means sniffing out opportunities and defining new projects for yourself in your current job.* What else needs to be done that interests you? What are the problems you can solve? Make projects for yourself that meet real needs in the company and boost your personal learning. Don't wait for someone to give you a project, make a project.

2. Ask yourself what you are selling.

Every worker sells something to the organization. It could be knowledge about software. It could be your sales skills, or your customer service skills, or the special relationships you have with clients. Make sure you have a clear picture of the specific value you bring to the firm.

Test yourself by asking if all you are selling is your time. If you could plug another warm body in your spot and no one would care, then you are vulnerable. Consider what you can bring to the job no one else can. What you sell is what keeps you around and keeps you growing.

3. Think of yourself as intellectual capital.

Intellectual capital is the business of selling ideas. If someone asked you what ideas you are selling, how would you answer? How to be a more effective bank teller? How to manage and motivate others? How to make a retail operation profitable? What is it that you know best, that characterizes you? That is your intellectual capital. And that is what you will offer companies now and in the future.

4. Then grow your intellectual capital.

Decide want you want to learn in your current job and decide what learning you want from a job in the future. I recently asked someone what kind of work he was looking for. He said, "Wherever I can get a good job." That's a bad answer. Good jobs are everywhere. Decide what you what to learn, what you want your expertise to be. You can always adjust and change your mind along the way. Just be sure you are growing your intellectual capital today.

How to Recognize a Genius Business Idea

The wisdom of the Sage is the knowledge of when they have a genius idea. Here are some clues to determine if you have a genius idea.

1. Find the yin and yang of simplicity and complexity.

At first glance a good idea seems powerfully simple, but upon closer examination, a quality idea grows larger. You see new applications of it; you envision more layers to it. Good ideas are both simple and complex.

2. Good ideas have a "third" meaning.

Sidney Lumet talks about knowing he has a great film when in the course of production the film takes on a third meaning; that is, some new storyline, subtext, or plot is born even as the film is being made. It has a life of its own.

So it is with genius business ideas. They have a life of their own. As you work with it, the idea becomes richer and has a momentum that draws others around it. It feels like you are following in the wake of the idea's boat. The idea is leading you. The dancer would say, "the dance dances you."

3. Someone important hates it.

Carl Jung said, "True genius intrudes and disrupts." If you don't intrude into the existing territory or disrupt the status quo, you don't have a breakthrough. So when you meet that inevitable opposition—"We can't do this because . . ." or, "So-and-so will never go for it . . ."—be thrilled. You've found a genius idea.

4. Be a midwife and a chaplain.

When an idea spreads through the firm, there will be new learning required from those who need to support it. If you don't hear growing pains in the organization, you may not have an idea worthy of the fight.

One business artist said she was hearing, " 'No, no, no, no' from every corner. I knew then that I just had to persevere in the face of 'No.' "

Every new idea causes a death. Learn to be a midwife—give birth to ideas. And learn to be a chaplain—bury the old ones. Good ideas stretch the capabilities of the organization.

5. Genius ideas are—in the end—elegant.

Scientists talk about ugly ideas—concepts that are awkward or thorny. Many ideas in business start as elegant and then we make them ugly. The purchasing department wants to do this to it. Legal wants to add this. Operations needs this. Sooner or later the idea looks like a gargoyle beast.

Strive to maintain the simple harmony, the balance, and intuitive rightness of the ideas. Keep your genius business ideas elegant.

III

Putting the Five Faces
of Genius to Work

*"We cannot will creativity. But we can will
to give ourselves to the encounter with
intensity of dedication and commitment."*

—ROLLO MAY

Each of us has moments in our careers when the headlights illuminate the road and we see the next stretch of highway ahead. These moments of enlightenment help us discover the terra incognita—the uncharted territory— of our business responsibilities and our creative lives.

Early in my career I experienced one of these moments. I told my supervisor we weren't going to make a project deadline. My list of limitations went on and on. The creative department was backed up. Even if we had the ads done, there wouldn't be enough time for production. The budget couldn't accommodate overtime. Every team member confirmed my suspicions. I tried to break the news to her gently, but I knew I was going to disappoint my supervisor and our client.

After patiently listening to me describe the problems, she said, "You haven't pushed the sides hard enough." I had no idea what she was talking about. I asked her, "Pushed what sides?" "The sides of the box." "What box?" "The box you're standing in."

She said every challenge is like standing in a box. My job was to push at each side of the box to see which side I could topple. Instead of accepting the limitations as constraints, I needed to find what I could do to change them. That creativity began when you refused to see the sides of the box as limitations but as potential windows into a radiant idea.

I don't really remember how I solved that problem, but I do remember hounding a team member with the perseverance of a Fool. I remember using the simplicity principle of the Sage to figure out the core problem. I used the Observer skill of curiosity. "Why does it have to be that way?" I had seen that map into terra incognita, the way toward solving the problem, and together the team made the deadline.

The Five Faces of Genius framework is a toolbox to help you blast through the walls of the box you're standing in. Imagine yourself with feet planted on the bottom of a box. Mark each wall and the ceiling with a Face of Genius. These are the metaconcepts—the thinking skills that are the way into the mystery of new ideas. Put them to work for you. Take on their full power. They can launch your genius within.

Now that you have been introduced to the Five Faces of Genius, you've seen how the skills of highly inventive people can help you with your own business challenges. This section is devoted to helping you master these skills every day, to become sensitive to the opportunities that appear, and to know when and how to use the skills in conjunction with one another. Remember: The goal is to master all five of the skills.

There are three steps you will need to take in order to get the most benefit out of the Five Faces. First, learn to use the Five Faces as a personal mental checklist. Second, use the framework to construct a more powerful team. Third, use the framework to spark your group's creative process. Let's deal first with the personal application.

Using the Five Faces of Genius as a Mental Checklist

We all have moments in our days when we are called upon to instantly solve a problem, come up with a creative idea, or figure out the next step. Occasionally an idea will come to us quickly, but often our creative tasks can be daunting and cause us stress. Sir Isaac Newton said the creative mind is "the mind voyaging through strange seas of thought alone." The Five Faces framework can help you navigate the seas of your imagination and grasp electric ideas.

Next time you are reaching for an idea—at your desk, in a meeting, in your car—start to mentally walk through the Five Faces of Genius. Let them be thinking companions. Five friends who stroll alongside you and ask you different questions:

THE SEER	What solutions do I see in my mind's eye?
THE OBSERVER	What do I notice around me that leads to a solution?
THE ALCHEMIST	What does this situation remind me of?
THE FOOL	What happens if I invert the situation? Come up with an absurd conclusion? What if I persevered?
THE SAGE	What simple solution could I create? What can I rekindle from the past?

Let's say that your creative profile tells you your dominant Face is that of a Sage. The primary way you create ideas is by simplifying problems and using the essence to invent. You also enjoy looking to the past for idea inspiration.

Let's also say that you need a name for a company. You have recently purchased a group of outpatient clinics and you want to create a name for the chain. These outpatient clinics provide urgent medical care to those in the surrounding community. The clinics are located throughout the suburban area of a large city. You want the name to be easily recognized and remembered. You want the name to connote quality health care, yet fast and friendly service.

THE SAGE

The first thing you do is simplify. The essence of the name should be quality health care—fast. You think of a name such as "QualCare Health Clinics."

THE SEER

You visualize. You see a picture in your mind's eye of a clinic, people walking through and getting treated quickly. You think of "Physicians On Call Clinics."

THE OBSERVER

During the description of the problem, you remember the smaller point of the clinics needing credibility. You decide to link the clinics to a larger hospital. You think of the name "QualCare Health Clinics: A Division of Providence General Hospital."

THE ALCHEMIST

The chain of clinics reminds you of the fast, quality service of an emergency room. You think of the name "Urgent Care Health Clinics."

THE FOOL

You think of the clinics that are often situated in a box like a strip mall. You invert the idea of the sterile, impersonal style of a clinic and name it "Your Family Doctor."

See how we rotated the problem and used all the Five Faces to examine possible creative outcomes? Knowing your profile helps you understand your first inclinations, but the framework opens up possibilities you would never have considered.

We mentioned earlier that the Five Faces of Genius are thinking skills or cognitive skills. Some cognitive skills overlap with personality styles more than others. This means that, depending on your primary creative style, some skills are more easily added to your toolbox than others.

Seers begin building mental pictures from early childhood. They easily find a picture and can often share it in great detail. Yet if you are not primarily a Seer, this is one of the more difficult skills to master. If you don't recognize yourself here, the Seer may be one skill to add once you've practiced others. Review the segment "Mastering the Seer at Work." But be patient with yourself. You can put the Seer on your back burner and tackle it a little later in your creative journey.

On the other hand, if you feel as if you have some affinity for the Seer, try practicing it right away. Sometimes folks do see pictures, but they don't realize their value until they notice the skill at work in creative genius. Once you decide it's worth paying attention to the pictures, you will be surprised how fruitful this skill can be. You'll likely find you can improve quickly and be pleased with your new energy for ideas.

The Fool's principles of inversion and absurdity also have a high overlap with personality. These folks grew up with a rich sense of humor. Yet surprisingly, the Fool skills are rather easy to learn. Most clients find inversion and absurdity refreshing approaches. They get good results from them right away. The Observer, Alchemist, and Sage are skills that are equally easy to embrace and have valuable outcomes.

Managers who are most successful in building their skills are those who finally believe creativity is their birthright, that they sell ideas, that ideas are what make us human. So, if you believe you can improve, you will improve. To affirm your own creativity is the critical first step toward your goal. You have the Face of Genius within.

Here's an example of how someone used the framework to creatively solve a business problem. Brian was the head of the new products team for a large food company. His team frequently came up with brilliant product ideas but found it difficult to get other departments excited about them. Without their support, Brian knew there was little chance his department would see their new products implemented.

Innovative products were the heart of Brian's company's long-term health. It was critically important to the financial success of the firm to develop new products and get them out in the market on a timely basis. Brian's goal was to launch three new products every year, and he had specific revenue goals attendant upon the success of these products.

Using the Five Faces, Brian walked through the problem and generated a list of possible ideas.

THE SEER

What solutions do you see in your mind's eye? If you could vision the wildly successful new products process, what would it look like?

One picture was of an inverted triangle through which product ideas trickle from the bottom up. What if more people were involved in the new products process? He considered a consortium approach that allowed for wider input and decision making across the leaders of the organization.

THE OBSERVER

Have you noticed any details lately that seemed significant? Any small influences that could lead to an idea?

In interviews with managers at the company, someone claimed the new products department's ideas didn't seem very innovative. Brian heard that reflected two more times. When he analyzed the department's process, he realized they were pre-screening ideas and eliminating the products they thought wouldn't fly within the company.

Another idea Brian generated was to create incentives for the new products team to consider the wilder ideas along with the safe ones.

THE ALCHEMIST

What analogies can lend insight? Are there models from other firms that can provide ideas?

A competing firm created a new ventures team that carries the full financial weight of developing prototypes and market testing them. Brian considered a reorganization of their firm to include a similar team, thus ensuring the new products would have the attention they needed.

THE FOOL

What if you inverted conventional wisdom? Are there absurd ideas to consider?

One inspiration was to kill the department altogether and to outsource all concept development for new products to a contract firm.

THE SAGE

How can you simplify the issue? When you distill the problem to its essence, what ideas do you find?

Then Brian simplified it. What if there was a "Fast Track" approval process with the presidents of each division that met regularly and tracked the progress of the chosen new product initiatives?

You can see how using the skills generates a wide range of alternative ideas to explore. The Five Faces of Genius becomes the mental checklist you need to expand your field of thinking. Instead of anchoring on one or two ideas, you can push at the frontiers of your imagination and develop more and higher quality ideas.

One truth we know underlies the creative process. That as you focus, commit, and strive to become more inventive, you will. *That effort is the prime mover of invention.* Creativity is at first a discipline. The discipline of the Five Faces of Genius is meant to be an entryway to the fertile land of your imagination. As Rollo May tells us, you cannot will to become more creative, but you can dedicate yourself to the endeavor. You can be a master of ideas.

Be aware that the biggest barrier to using the Five Faces of Genius framework as a mental checklist is the Hurry Scurry Syndrome. Again, when we notice a creative challenge, we try to solve it fast—hurry; or we find someone to run to—scurry.

A frequent outcome of the Hurry Scurry Syndrome is to think "Let's get the team!" We feel more comfortable in the mystery of the unknown when we have a couple colleagues around us. But to be an idea leader you need to have the courage to make the Five skills a mental habit. Try to generate your own unique ideas before bringing in others. You'll find you build your confidence in your creative spirit.

Some clients say to me, "But my ideas are not as important as getting the team to agree," and I say, "Are you sure?" Are you sure the team can really generate better ideas? Are you sure the team's agreement will really affect the quality of the ideas you generate? Are you sure that if you didn't do a little advance work, your ideas—yours and the team's—would be better?

I have discovered that *corporations rely too heavily on teams for innovation.* I consistently find corporations substitute team process for personal creativity. Brainstorming meetings are euphemisms for "Don't Worry About Preparing" meetings. People come to meetings expecting an angel of invention to land on their shoulder, but teams can become an excuse for avoiding individual creative work and a crutch to gain internal consensus. The team orientation of many corporate cultures can reflect the bias of implementation over imagination.

Ideas come to people individually and not to teams. Teams may facilitate, build, or implement ideas, but the spark of ingenuity strikes in units of one. We need to master our own imagination first, learn how it works, and then master its use in teams. Then we can ask what is the role of teams and how can we make ideas come to life in groups.

At the beginning of the book, I told you creativity demands your soul. Search your soul to determine if you are using your full capacities as a creative individual or if you are overrelying on others.

So, then, the easiest way to master the Five Faces of Genius is to commit them to memory. That way you always have them with you. Learn to trust your creative spirit first—your mental back pocket. This is how they become a second skin. You'll want to remember these easy handles:

THE SEER	See it.
THE OBSERVER	Notice it.
THE ALCHEMIST	Mix it.
THE FOOL	Celebrate it.
THE SAGE	Simplify it.

This shorthand will remind you of the skills no matter where you are. The commands prod to get you into your imagination and onto ideas.

Earlier we talked about creating the solitude and space to practice these skills in the course of your work. Here's a ritual to adopt that will help you use the framework as your mental checklist:

❑ **Carve out five minutes for self-reflection.**
Find a place to be alone. Isolate yourself in your car or an empty conference room. Take a walk outdoors.

❑ **Define the issue, challenge, or opportunity.**
What is it you are trying to solve? Think of the issue in as big and broad terms as possible.

❑ **Run through the discipline of the Five Faces of Genius.**
Ask yourself the questions listed on page 143. Start with your dominant Face. Then progress to the other four. What ideas surface? If you can, jot down your ideas in a journal or on a notepad.

❑ **Use the framework again.**
Go through the practice of each Face. You'll find the second time through uncovers even deeper ideas.

You may tend to lean on your dominant creative style at first and keep simplifying like a Sage or asking yourself about the details you've noticed like an Observer. This is very natural. Most of us have to work at branching out. If it makes it easier for you, try to select one or two new skills to add to your inquiry. Work at them individually and practice. Use the summary chart to remind yourself of the ways you wanted to master the Faces. Soon you will find you have one or two new skills in your toolbox.

As you become more familiar, you will be able to use the framework as a mental checklist in the presence of others. While you are thinking and dreaming in conversations or in meetings, you'll be able to create the mindspace to practice the framework. A client said, "While I'm jogging, new ideas come. Then I augment those by starting the Five Faces of Genius engine. It helps me figure out if I've explored all the options. What have I missed?" So as you begin, you'll get there faster if you work alone. The Five Faces of Genius requires a moment of concentrated reflection.

Another client said the Five Faces of Genius framework helps him "firefight." Like most of us, he is running at work, trying to squelch the current day's problem. And when the challenges come, he feels they require "creativity under pressure." This is when the framework helps him best. When he's rushed and under pressure, he tries to find some concentrated mind time and runs through the Five Faces. This is how his radiant ideas are born. Even when you are rushed and under pressure, you can still invent.

One of the best employees I ever had was a master of her imagination. When our team would meet for creative solutions, she came prepared with one or two ideas to share. It was obvious she had cleared the mental space to think about the problem in advance, and her personal advance work primed the team for great collaborative thinking.

Once you make a regular practice of the framework, you will be well on your way to becoming a business artist. You'll find ideas to share, and when you meet with your teams, you'll be one step ahead and able to take the role of creative leader.

Some wonder if they should spend more time developing their strengths or improving their weaknesses. For example, if I write down the Seer and Sage as my primary skills, should I work on improving those or concentrate on the other three Faces?

The answer depends on you. If you feel sure of your strengths, it is more beneficial to tackle some new skills. Try to expand. Add another Face. However, if you feel tentative in the selection of your dominant skills, focus on enhancing your primary skills, or one that particularly attracts you. Just don't focus on one or two and forget about the others. They may be friends you never took the time to make.

See if you can expand your repertoire and include all the skills. You will find you use them at different times and under different circumstances. How might you incorporate some Fool skills? How might you improve your ability to become an Alchemist? Make the effort to put the entire basket of tools at your mental disposal.

Creating Business Sabbaticals

A sabbatical is a practice academics and thinkers have used for centuries to rejuvenate their creative spirit. It's time off to reflect, research, recharge. Time to rest, recommit, rethink. Now, you may not be able to get away for three months, but the sabbatical concept can be reconfigured for the twenty-first century.

Increasingly, business artists are building sabbaticals into their schedule. Here's how:

1. Get unplugged.

Schedule time in your calendar to think. Go somewhere that inspires you. Don't take a cell phone. Put an extended absence greeting on your voice mail. Turn off your pager. Technological improvements may not be improvements for your business artistry. Occasionally get rid of them.

Once you get to the place of inspiration—your car, your home, the library, the cafeteria—just think. Let your mind wander. Let yourself be alone with imagination without interruption.

2. Find a "seed sorting" project.

Monks in the religious traditions did handwork to wait for inspiration. They sorted seeds, baked bread, worked in the garden. Inspiration for our business challenges happens when we focus on something other than the problem.

Find a project at work that lets your mind wander. It's a mental sabbatical. Create a small garden or enjoy a computer game. Some business artists keep jigsaw puzzles in their office to work on. Some even bring knitting to meetings. Increase the probability of inspiration by keeping your hands busy while you think.

3. Dance every twenty minutes.

Dance! The best-selling author Rebecca Wells, who wrote *The Divine Secrets of the Ya-Ya Sisterhood*, said she timed her writing and got up every twenty minutes to dance. Get away from your desk or your meetings. Stretch, chat, relax every twenty minutes. It will give you energy. And surplus energy leads to ideas.

4. Make a makeshift office.

For a two- or three-day stretch, try moving your office to another location. This location could be your dining room table. It could be a library, a park bench, or a coffee shop. Tell your colleagues you are on a minisabbatical. Bring a cell phone for occasional check-ins. You'll get a lot done.

5. Plan rests.

Every three months, take a few days of true rest. Think about life. This is not vacation. This is not errand time. This is life work. Relax, regroup, and dream. You never know what life directions you will discover. Mother Teresa had a vision for her future while riding on a train at the age of thirty-seven. African-American preachers in some Pentecostal traditions pray for three days for a vision from God. As Rollo May says, "Waiting requires a high degree of attention." Pay attention for inspiration.

6. Consider a traditional sabbatical.

A business artist found herself between projects in her firm. Rather than worry she needed to get "busy" right away, she asked her management for a three-month leave with no pay but health benefits. She used the time to rest, visit family, play, and live a little. She explored what she wanted in her career. Set goals. Planned. She came back to the job with more energy and a renewed commitment.

You may even find that your management is open to paid sabbaticals. Consider crafting a research project that invigorates you and brings fresh information back to the firm. Could you find out what's new in other sales organizations? Could you research the Internet's influence on your company's future? What would be fascinating to you and worthwhile to those around you? Grow your intellectual capital. At the end of the day, that's all you really have to sell. Be bold.

Using the Five Faces of Genius to Construct Teams

The second way to use the framework is by identifying how to best work together. Most of us are required to work with a team or group every day. The Five Faces of Genius offers a great way to understand your group members and how you can best work together. Here's how to begin.

You have already identified your own creative profile. Now assess the creative styles of the individuals of your team. It's relatively easy to pick out the styles of your co-workers. We spend so much time with them that we can almost predict how our bosses, co-workers, and subordinates will navigate their imagination and respond to the ideas of others. In fact, sometimes we are more aware of their creative process than we are of our own.

A client noted how difficult it was to work with his boss. "It seems when I have just made up my mind about how I will proceed on a problem, Frank likes to come in and bust things up—even when I have more information about what is going on; even when I am closer to the problem. He finds a way to flip things around. It's as if he rejoices in screwing up my plans. Not that I don't like him—I do. And once we work together, he usually has some spark to add to my decisions. Since I've been exposed to the Five Faces of Genius, I realize this isn't Frank's *management* style as much as it is his *creative* style. He is a classic Fool. The way he processes ideas is to invert or push things to the absurd. Now that I know this, I understand him better and have come up with ways to welcome his improvements to my ideas." Once we understand our colleagues better, it helps to feed that intimacy of imagination we will talk about shortly, which makes for dynamic teams.

Because we usually have a "one-skill habit," you can often guess the primary style of your colleagues. Use the descriptions in the Five Faces chapters to identify their styles. Or you can expose them to the ideas in this book and ask them to identify their own styles. Either way, determine the configuration of the creative profiles in the group. Survey the team and find the Faces of Genius present.

The best creative teams are those that have all Five Faces represented in the group. When you have all the creative styles reflected in your group, you can examine multiple pathways into ideas. When each person masters one of the principles, you can use your talents in concert. The Seer will be visualizing potential outcomes and describing possible ways to get there.

The Observer will be collecting the details that can give way to ideas. The Alchemist will be looking for possible connections to other domains. The Fool will be turning the challenge upside down, and the Sage will be using the heart of the matter as creative fire. Together the Five Faces of Genius are a dynamic combination that can lead to successful and fufilling business artistry.

The only dysfunctional group of Faces is one dominated by one or two single creative profiles—made up of all Alchemists, all Sages, for example. They are so similar that collaboration is painful and the quality of the group's ideas suffers. We talk in business about diversity—appreciating racial diversity, ethnic diversity, gender diversity, and more. It's time to appreciate creative diversity. There is power gleaned from differing creative strengths. It is in the exploitation of diverse skills that large ideas lie.

Getting all Five Faces represented in a work team can be challenging. Different industries, firms, disciplines, and even different departments within firms have higher concentrations of different Faces. For example, research-and-development teams that hire engineers have a higher percentage of Observers. They use their analytical skills to collect data and draw inventive inferences from it. Salespeople have more Seers in their ranks. Alchemists are sprinkled in different disciplines but are idea leaders in many functions. To get a mix of Faces in your group, you may have to investigate outside your immediate work team or consider hiring employees with different backgrounds than you normally might.

If it's impossible to find a group with diverse profiles, then the team needs to work together to improve the collective weaknesses. You can learn more about this below in the "Using the Five Faces of Genius for a Group Creative Process" segment.

Using the Five Faces of Genius for a Group Creative Process

There are two kinds of groups you work with in corporate life: political and intimate. Political systems consist of those people with whom you regularly interact—co-workers, customers, colleagues, clients. These are people you serve, who may not be directly invested in the success of your work; in fact, you may be competing with these folks for position or influence.

Intimate systems are those two to five people you know well at work. You care about them. They care about you. You may be in competition with them for position or influence, but you respect them enough to battle with them. These are the people whom you click with about ideas, goals, direction of your work. These are the people who make working where you do worth it.

Much work that demands creative solutions in an organization happens in political settings, such as work teams, large brainstorming sessions, and department meetings. Most managers are familiar with these groups, but political groups are not the place for genuinely creative exploration. People are trying to impress each other with their imaginative largesse. Others are trying to drive the decision maker to buy their idea. Invention needs a safe haven. When working on truly creative endeavors, strive to work with a more intimate team.

I encourage clients to stop big brainstorming sessions or strategy meetings and concentrate on developing intimate creative partnerships of two to five people. Each business artist is smart enough to decide who they need in that group to be more innovative and to make their ideas fly. These small groups operate on intimate interpersonal systems and not political ones. They learn to trust each other. Accept one another's failures and learn to respect and value one another's diverse creative styles. Ideally these people should have a strong representation of all the Five Faces of Genius—folks who have an arsenal of thinking skills available to them. Because brainstorming with large groups is a throwback to the old economy. In the new economy of ideas, intimate creative partnerships rule the day.

BECAUSE ALL INSPIRATION IS AT ITS CORE A SOLITARY PROCESS

Whether in an artist's studio or a corporate conference room, ideas strike individuals. We need to make sure we have time alone in the course of our business day. Time for the muse of invention to strike. Make time for a little solitude and navigate your imagination. Master the Five Faces of Genius framework on your own before you try to master it in the context of your team. Innovation starts with *your* personal genius. You can become a leader, someone on whom the group relies for creativity when you commit to a life of ideas.

Getting Groups to Big Ideas

Here are some suggestions for getting beyond brainstorming for group creative process. Business artists help others navigate their imaginations as a group. Here's how:

1. Keep your group small—very small.

I remember a brainstorming session that had thirty people present. What a nightmare. People were trying to grandstand their creativity like circus ringleaders.

It's hard to exclude people from meetings. Sue comes from operations. Joe from sales. Your boss, your colleagues' bosses. The people who report to you. The people you wish reported to you. Soon there are way too many people. In order to be a team player, you end up compromising the quality of the ideas.

A good creative process requires no more than five people. Strive for a very small group of two to five people. Find your business "intimates." Try to include those who reflect all the creative styles of the Five Faces of Genius.

2. Encourage folks to come to meetings with kernels to share.

In advance, give folks an idea of what you would like to accomplish in your meeting. Give them an agenda. Explain the issue and then provide questions that they should personally answer before attending. This gives people time to commit the issue to their memory and to prepare for the creative process. Encourage them to use the Five Faces of Genius process in advance.

3. Separate strategy discussion and ideation.

The primary force that derails the creative process is dissension about the task. When folks disagree about what problem you are trying to solve, the meeting fails.

Try to get consensus in advance about the meeting purpose. If you can get agreement, use your first meeting to clarify the issue and then set another meeting to create ideas. Consider calling a meeting for fact sharing and a second meeting for creative process.

Strategy and ideation often require two sets of mental skills. Strategy tends to be linear and critical. Ideation is noncritical and wideminded. Few managers can shift gears quickly and easily. Separate the processes to get the best results.

4. Provide something messy—and I don't mean donuts.

Are you trying to figure out how to improve customer service? Come in with a complaint letter from a customer to read. Are you trying to develop an idea for a new software product? Ask an end user to come in and talk with you about their needs. Trying to figure out how to respond to a competitor? Bring in their latest product. Start your meetings with some real stimulus. Give people something practical to chew on. It primes the pump of invention.

5. Be the idea champion.

Don't just expect magic to happen because you ask people to show up. Keep the creative momentum moving. Plan a schedule of exercises that will help you toward your goal. Consider using some of the Five Faces of Genius exercises featured in each of the Face chapter segments devoted to teams. Navigating ideas requires a leader. Let it be you.

6. Start a "brain trust."

Find two to five people and develop a creative "brain trust." When issues need to be solved, get the same people in the room. Develop an ongoing relationship. Understand where each fits in the Five Faces profiles. Figure out how your creative styles work together.

If you build a relationship over time, you'll have higher success in developing breakthrough ideas. You'll learn to rely on one another, trust one another, and understand how you work together. This is your safe haven for exploration.

7. Recognize that creating ideas and selling ideas require two different skill sets.

Corporate culture uses brainstorming sessions to sell ideas. The conventional wisdom is that when people participate in meetings, they will own the ideas developed. Sometimes this works, but mostly it doesn't. In a meeting of thirty people, you will rarely sell anything. Study how to sell creative ideas. A start will be "How to Sell Inspired Ideas" on page 165.

HOW THE FACES RELATE
TO ONE ANOTHER

You can predict dynamic combinations within teams and avoid trouble spots by knowing which styles work together best. When you know the creative profile of your team members, you can communicate about ideas and navigate the mystery of your business more effectively together.

POWERFUL PARTNERSHIPS

SEERS AND ALL FACES

Seers partner well with most of the Faces of Genius. I have a colleague who calls Seers the "O positive blood." Their creative style mixes well with everyone. Seers use their visual pictures to test the outcomes of the group's concepts. The team relies upon the Seer to help the group visualize the creative paths where the business may go.

OBSERVERS AND SEERS

Observers paired with Seers is a particularly fertile combination. The Observers unearth the detail, posit great solutions, and then the Seer visualizes potential outcomes for each. Together they can develop tremendous ideas. Strive to find a Seer–Observer pair within your group.

ALCHEMISTS AND OBSERVERS

Alchemists are pleasures in a team. They have lots of good ideas. Their analogies fire the creative spirit of others. Because Alchemists are triggered by dialogue, they love group expression and ideation. They have the most enthusiasm for the team creative model. Remember that Alchemists ideate from similarities and Observers from differences. The combination of Alchemists and Observers can be powerful.

SAGES AND FOOLS

Sages make good creative partners with Fools. The Sage respects the ideas of the Fool. They sense the "dead on" nature of the Fool's genius and often find a way to make the Fool's idea fly further in the context of an organization. Sages clear a path for the Fool's ideas. The Fool likes the fact that the Sage won't mess with their central idea and won't try to frill it up or fix it.

POTENTIAL CONFLICTS

OBSERVERS AND SAGES

Observers and Sages can ruffle each other's feathers. Sages lose patience with Observers who get their ideas by collecting data points. While the Observer likes input, the Sage is trying to coalesce and simplify. Yet when they forge a relationship that works, they can help each other. The Sage brings the insight the Observer likes, and the Observer helps keep the Sage from eliminating too much. Make sure mutual respect wins out.

ALCHEMISTS AND ALL FACES

Because the alchemists' creative style relies on analogy, they can depend too much on the dynamics of the group. While waiting for good experiences to draw on, the Alchemist burns through the creative fuel of their team and then wants to look beyond team members' contributions. Those who work with Alchemists or have an Alchemist as a supervisor need to constantly be refreshing their stimulus for ideas. Like farmers who rotate crops, Alchemists like to rotate the stimulus around them.

FOOLS AND ALL FACES

Fools' creative process is particularly solitary. They have their own great ideas and want the rest of the group to follow. They don't like to morph ideas and change their shape, so teams are not their favorite venue. Yet because of the quality of their ideas, it's important to keep them around and engaged. Import the gifts of the Fool from other parts of the firm or hire outside talent. Try to keep at least one Fool in your group. Check on page 107 for ideas on how to nurture Fools in teams.

The key to making teams great is knowing where you are weak—what creative profiles you lack—and then working to remedy the imbalance.

When I worked with Roberto, he was trying to improve the creative output of his team. He was a manager of a group of engineers in the research division of a technology firm. "We are not very innovative together. We get stuck a lot. It seems the same people offer ideas and then we have trouble building on them. How can we create a sense of *dynamism* together?"

Roberto asked each manager in the group to take the Five Faces of Genius profile. What he found astounded him. Out of the seven managers, four were primarily Observers. As you remember, Observers collect data and use the data as a springboard for ideas. They can find it difficult to get to the data they need in a group process. Roberto was an Alchemist. His "conversational" environment was highly important, and he needed stimulus from others to bounce ideas back and forth. The lone Sage and Seer felt like fish out of water. The Observers' quiet way made them feel as though no one understood their ideas.

Roberto and I set about a plan to reconfigure the group to augment the creative styles of the team and be sure all Five Faces were represented. One of the engineers wanted to transfer to the wireless division. Roberto had been fighting it because the engineer was talented and Roberto wanted to keep him, but now realized the move might better suit the team. Roberto replaced him with Keith, a talented engineer who had Fool skills. Keith was able to turn problems around and was very verbal and prolific with ideas. Keith, the Fool, and the Sage in the group developed a creative spark and began working together, frequently presenting the team with more ideas.

Roberto found Sheila, a Seer who was a creative leader, in the manufacturing division. He asked if Sheila could sit in on some of their key meetings and help to provide creative vision. Sheila knew the research function well and had an investment in innovation. Now there was a Seer who could partner with the other Seer and build on the Observers' ideas. With just two moves, Roberto had changed the internal dynamics enough to turn around the creative energy of the group. "Now we are a well-oiled machine. I was surprised how much our creative styles determine how we work as a team."

Remember to use the Five Faces model to help assess the strengths and weaknesses of your team. You'll find there are some easy ways you can make your group complete and begin navigating the business opportunity together.

As I said, there are two ways you can augment your team, by adding new members or through intentional team exercises. When you find it impossible to change the members of your group, work hard on these team exercises. You can easily bring a new dimension to the quality of your team work. Now, let's dig deeper and discuss using all five skills in a group.

Just as the Five Faces of Genius framework unlocks ideas as a personal mental checklist, you can also use it in the context of a team. You can think of the framework as a *group* checklist.

When you've determined the nature of your challenge, you can lead meetings by guiding the group through the Five Faces of Genius queries from page 143. Lead them through the questions individually or choose one or two that seem most appropriate to challenge the team. Begin with the questions and then discuss potential solutions.

Further, you can use the exercises described in the Five Faces of Genius chapter segments or even create exercises of your own around the thinking skills. Ask the group to join you in exploring the exercises. This way the entire team gets to practice the skills. It gives a fresh approach to typical meetings. You'll find people's sense of their own creativity heightened and an excitement about a new perspective.

Remember my colleague who always came to team meetings with good ideas? The other quality that made her a business artist was that she could lead the group into new ideas. Instead of fixating on the ideas she brought, she asked questions that helped all of us navigate our imaginations together.

When teams find they have other options besides brainstorming, they breath a sigh of relief. Brainstorming can be frustrating and create tension in individuals. People want new ways to navigate their business imagination. New skills give folks a boost up the hill of invention. One client says, "We put posters of each of the Five Faces of Genius principles around our conference room. During meetings we share ideas we've developed using the framework. It gives us a jump start."

One of the biggest barriers to group process is that most managers don't feel creative. Fear permeates the meeting. The anxiety about whether or not we can make a creative contribution runs high. Added to that is the anxiety about the task itself. The business issue that needs to be addressed carries its own weight. We worry that if we don't have a good idea, it will threaten our firm, our jobs, or us. So there are usually a few strikes against us as we begin.

By designing questions for your team, you can lance the pressure many feel. You can give the team's brain an oxygen hit. The business artist marshals the collective anxiety of the group and puts it to creative use.

Ask folks what solutions they see in their mind's eye. Ask them to share their wildly successful outcomes and envision the steps to get there. Ask them to identify the conventional wisdom around the issue and then invert it or push it to its extreme. Ask them to distill the problem to its essence. What is the heart of it? What ideas are born? When you demonstrate confidence in your imagination, you boost the confidence of the team.

How to Sell Inspired Ideas

For holiday gifts, I'm tempted to give my husband things that *I* really want for the house. I figure he'll enjoy the new duvet cover as much as I will. Or the mixer. Or the new couch. But I have to stop and remind myself that good gift givers don't do that. The trick to making someone happy is figuring out what the other really wants, and as is within your means, getting it for them.

Selling ideas is like good gift giving. Figuring out what the other person wants and then using your creative resources to meet their needs.

The key to selling ideas is framing ideas in terms of the benefits to others. Decide who are the important audiences for your idea and then turn the best face of the idea toward that audience. Here are some guidelines to follow:

1. Think of your idea as a "gift" to the other.

What does your boss, your customer, your co-worker really want or need? Find the overlap between what they need and your idea. When you "unwrap" the idea and explain it to your audience, be sure to unveil that side of the idea first.

2. Expect resistance.

All great ideas bring a death to the organization and some folks work hard to kill ideas that threaten the status quo. Try to figure out who will resist you and then make a specific plan to address their concerns.

3. Find one unusual ally.

Share your idea with someone you respect yet who doesn't have a direct stake in it. Ask for advice on how to craft your concept, how to make it bigger, and how to sell it.

4. Find a more unusual ally.

Share the idea with someone you know will hate it but who doesn't have a direct stake in it. Ask for advice on how to craft your concept, how to make it bigger, and how to sell it.

5. Consider the maverick.

If you were a maverick and didn't much care what others thought, how would you approach people within the organization. Remember that everyone will not like this idea. Recognize it early and decide who you can afford to alienate and who you can't.

6. Pay attention to ideas you are not selling.

If you find your ideas are rarely accepted or implemented, it may say more about you than the organization. Check your selling style, the quality of your ideas. Practice idea landscaping (introduced on page 171). Remember: Part of being a creative person is learning to adapt and change.

7. Become an Easter bunny.

One business artist uses the "Easter bunny" model for selling ideas. He informally visits colleagues and drops "eggs" or ideas in their office. With each visit, he describes the idea in a way that highlights the unique benefits for that person. In this sense, he canvasses, or presells, the ideas and gives people time to accept them as their own.

Start regular "I have an idea" conversations with those around you. Share your ideas with your boss, customers, other business artists, peers—anyone who will listen. Get recognized as someone who invents.

8. Study a salesperson.

Sales is a mighty craft. Analyze it. Read books about it. Make a friend of a salesperson. Figure out what skills you can use for selling your ideas.

Study the movie *12 Angry Men*. This classic directed by Sidney Lumet highlights the ability of one man to open the minds of eleven angry colleagues in a jury. Here you'll find the highest expression of persuasion in action.

9. Get to the highest level you can.

It's hard to determine who will be the person who can make your ideas fly. We often find our ideas don't get elevated to the right people who have the authority to make them happen. Think hard about who the right people are and how to get to them. Sometimes it's possible to short-circuit the protocol to get to the right people. Remember the Hewlett-Packard executive who took his idea and presented it to customers without internal approval. The idea sold itself.

HOW TO BUILD INTIMATE CREATIVE PARTNERSHIPS

At times we help developing intimate creative partnerships. How do we start that process of working with another for the best ideas?

RULE ONE

Understand the creative profile of your colleague. Do some behind-the-scenes evaluation. Try to determine what skill they use most frequently. If they took the "Five Faces of Genius Profiler," how might they answer? Or read the segments on understanding each Face of Genius. Where might you place your co-worker?

As I said earlier, most managers have a "one-skill habit." That means that they overuse one of the creative styles. This is their dominant face, and they may not be aware they use only one. They do not realize they have only one tool in the toolbox. As an idea leader, it's your job to help them to branch out and expand their portfolio of skills to enter into the world of ideas. What are the skills of your audience?

RULE TWO

Try to meet them on their ground. Let them know you understand their style. If they are an Alchemist, start using analogies to describe ideas. If they are a Seer, start using pictures to describe ideas. You don't need to make it obvious. Don't say, "I'm going to use Alchemist skills like yours." Just casually acknowledge you understand them by occasionally thinking as they do in front of them. Unconsciously, they will begin to feel that you know how they work—you understand their imagination—and they will begin to feel more comfortable sharing ideas with you. You'll develop that intimate system I mentioned earlier that undergrids good creative process.

RULE THREE

Let them watch you try on new skills. When they can see you risk and step out of your one-skill habit, it gives your colleagues renewed strength that they can do it. You can say, "This may lead me nowhere, but I'm going to try to look at the opposite of the situation and see what ideas I might generate." Then start using the Fool skills, for instance, and see what happens. When they watch you risk and fail and not be ashamed, they may be willing to learn from you and take your lead.

Sometimes we find ourselves working with folks who are not very confident in their creative skills. They are shy about sharing new ideas. These folks especially need to be able to see you try on new skills; see you risk and fail and watch you flounder. The intimacy will be born only when you are vulnerable with them. It may help to say, "You know, sometimes I don't feel very creative myself. I just figure that even a blind squirrel will find an acorn once in a while. I believe it pays to keep trying."

Occasionally managers are confronted with powerful people who believe their ideas are always best. These powerful personalities find it difficult to reach out, truly listen, and consider the ideas of others. How can you be heard? How can you make sure your ideas are given the airtime they deserve?

When this happens to us, the obvious place to lay blame is with the powerful personality. We say, "They just don't listen and they need to pay attention to others' ideas. They need to recognize that good ideas come from everywhere and everyone—even if they are not in a position of power in the organization." But surprisingly, I find the person who doesn't feel heard shares a portion of that blame. Let me explain.

Earlier I said that creative partnerships in business happen in intimate systems: I trust you to listen to my ideas and I trust that you will hear mine. You'll give me honest feedback and I'll tell you the truth. We'll share stupid ideas. We'll share radiant ideas. We'll learn to commune in that mystery together in which we are not sure where we're going, but we hope it leads to something.

What often happens is the powerful personality is looking for a creative partnership, but the other isn't prepared to offer it. The person who doesn't feel heard goes to the "powerful one" and wants to have their idea rubber-stamped—accepted—but the powerful personality smells this like a bad perfume. The colleague doesn't exhibit confidence in their idea. Perhaps they don't even exhibit confidence in their creative spirit. The "powerful" one needs to know the other truly believes the idea has merit and should be considered. Remember, in an intimate creative partnership, the power doesn't rest in your partner's acceptance of the idea. The power rests in the idea itself. If it's a good idea, you'll both believe it.

I had a client who felt as though her boss never really took her ideas seriously. She complained that when it came time to solve complicated problems, her boss would confide in another subordinate and not in her. And when she did share ideas, her boss didn't accept them. When I asked my client whether she believed she had ideas to contribute, she said, "If I was included more, I'd have more ideas." What she was saying is that she lacked the confidence to be a partner; that she needed the boss to validate her first and then her ideas would come. In fact, it works the other way around. When we start believing in our ideas and the power of our creative energy, we become recognized as someone worthy of partnership. As this client practiced her facility with ideas, her confidence grew and she became a more valued member of the team and a more vital presence to her boss.

If you find yourself looking for a creative partnership with a powerful personality, three approaches can be very valuable. First, go back and study the skills of the Fool. Make friends with a Fool. Learn to fight with the persistence your ideas deserve. When you know you are right, don't back down. Powerful people will not recognize you unless you believe you deserve to be heard. They honor the ones who lay it on the line, who go back again and again, who don't mind being bloodied by the battle. Be smart about what you can compromise, but compromise when you know you'll never win.

Second, work hard at mastering all Five Faces. When you have the confidence in your ability to think creatively, you'll bolster your confidence in your creative spirit. Remember you have the birthright of creativity. The final chapter will help you in this regard. In an intimate creative partnership, it's okay to doubt your idea. *But you cannot doubt the power of your creative spirit.* Become the creative business colleague you would like to have—the one who believes in their power to create something from nothing, who knows meaning in work comes from vital contributions. These are the people powerful people want beside them.

Last, study the section on selling ideas and the next notion of idea landscaping. You'll find more suggestions on how to frame ideas in terms of benefits to others. This goes a long way toward ensuring your ideas will be heard.

Mastering Idea Landscaping to Sell Ideas at Work

Selling ideas within the context of an organization can be challenging. But the Five Faces of Genius offers a pathway to making sure your ideas see the light of day.

This segment describes how to frame ideas for colleagues. Idea landscaping is the notion that if you share your ideas in the same way someone else creates their own ideas, you will have a better chance of being understood. How can you use *their* creative style to ensure they understand *your* concept?

The key to selling creative ideas is helping another recognize the idea's benefit in a way they understand. When your listener can navigate with you and use *their* imagination and creative thinking tools in your presence, you've opened the door.

Let's landscape an idea for each Face so that you can see how each works in conversation with a hypothetical supervisor.

Imagine you manage a number of call centers for a direct-marketing catalog firm. Customers call in and order apparel and other items. Recently you've been experiencing an unusually high number of calls and you're concerned you don't have enough operators to handle them. You need to sell your supervisor a creative solution to answering the overflow calls at the telecommunication center.

LANDSCAPING IDEAS FOR SEERS

You've read the Five Faces of Genius chapters. You believe your boss may be a Seer. He likes to talk in terms of pictures. He frequently says, "It looks like this . . ." when describing his thoughts or ideas. For him a picture speaks a million words.

You begin describing your idea by drawing a picture of the present situation.

YOU: Can we discuss the call volume problem in Atlanta? I think I have some ideas on how to solve it.

SEER BOSS: Sure. I'd like to see what you have.

YOU: Let me paint a picture of this problem. Imagine a new call coming into the center, say our Atlanta center. It's a new customer ready to order. She is ready to spend three hundred dollars or more on our merchandise. The caller gets the "Please hold" greeting. She holds for thirty seconds; one minute. Can you see her frustration? The caller is exasperated. She wiggles in her chair. The caller begins to question whether she really wants to spend the money. Two minutes. She is livid. She hangs up.

SEER BOSS: How often do you imagine that happens?

YOU: We project about ten percent of the time. Here's what I think might work.

SEER BOSS: Continue.

YOU: Now, picture this scenario. We've hired an overflow service. Another caller who is ready to spend three hundred dollars. She gets the "Please hold" greeting. Fifteen seconds later she is connected to a customer service rep. The sale is made. Let me show you this chart. If ten percent of our calls are hang-ups, that means we have one thousand lost calls per week. With the profit we make on that extra revenue, we could more than pay for the cost of the service.

SEER BOSS: I can already imagine the ways we could use that extra profit.

Notice when we landscape an idea for the Seer, we draw a visual picture. We use language that reinforces their power of visualization. We show visual stimulus like a graph. *We frame our idea in terms of a picture.*

LANDSCAPING IDEAS FOR OBSERVERS

When presenting an idea to an Observer, the first task is to explain your investigative process. Observers are as interested in *how* you got your idea as the idea itself. Observers want to know you've done a good job collecting the right details. Are they relevant? Why? Did you neglect some influences? What were they? Observers want to hear the means and the ends of your idea. The wisdom is knowing how much and what to include. Don't over-do it.

Second, explain your creative hypotheses. Which ideas did you consider? Give them two or three options. Give them the texture of the idea. Observers like to have a few details laid out. Be prepared to present a few different ways your idea will work.

Your discussion with an Observer boss might go something like this:

YOU:	A few weeks ago, I got a call from the Atlanta center. The floor manager thought he was getting into a chronic overload situation. I decided to check it out further.
OBSERVER BOSS:	What data did you collect?
YOU:	Over the next three weeks we analyzed every time there was an overload. Calls were on hold for an average of one minute for fifty-five percent of the time. I also ran the same analysis in the Denver and San Francisco locations. Calls were on hold over one minute for forty percent of the time.
OBSERVER BOSS:	I'm curious. What percentage of the calls waiting hung up?
YOU:	About five percent. That calculates to about $550,000 in lost revenue per week.
OBSERVER BOSS:	Ouch. Are you sure you've got all the relevant information?
YOU:	Here's a report of research methods for you to review. Here are my best ideas how to resolve this. One: We could hire more people to handle overflow calls. I've got the

numbers for this if you're interested. Two:
We could open another facility in Seattle. I
have an analysis for when this would be
possible for us. Three: And this is my
recommendation. Hire a contract firm to
handle the temporary overload. This will
bring the call-overload volume to one to two
percent short-term at a reasonable cost.
Here's a spreadsheet for you to analyze my
recommendation. We can reevaluate in three
months. What have I missed that you
noticed?

First, we talked about the process of analyzing the problem—who we talked to, what data we collected. We gave the boss the relevant details. This gives the Observer confidence that you have fully considered the process.

Next, when we presented our creative ideas, we gave alternatives to consider as well as a recommendation, with more detail available in written form. And finally, we explained when to reevaluate.

The most common mistake people make when working with Observers is jumping into the ideas without enough background. This makes Observers nervous. They like to be sure they are inventing around the right problem.

LANDSCAPING IDEAS FOR ALCHEMISTS

The first rule in successfully communicating ideas to Alchemists is dialogue. They eagerly want to share with you what they think. They want give and take. Their imagination sparks during dialogue. It isn't difficult to get an Alchemist talking about ideas.

Remember that the point of idea landscaping is to imagine together. You serve the creative process best if you use the Alchemists' bevy of ideas as a springboard to discovery. It's important to be genuinely interested in the content of their ideas, and then build together. Be sure to include your own ideas.

Alchemists are dependent upon you, the creative partner. For the Alchemist, it's in the talking that their idea comes to life. They need someone who will hear them. They rely on you. And it can become a source of insecurity in their imaginative process.

One helpful technique when describing ideas for the Alchemist is to reveal your creative idea and let them build on it. Your dialogue about the overload calls at the telecommunications center might go something like this:

YOU: I suppose you've heard about the call-overload situation at the Denver telecommunications center.

ALCHEMIST BOSS: Yes, I've been wondering what to do about it. Last time, we hired a contract service to handle the call overload, but we had quality-control issues. Their staff wasn't as well trained as ours.

YOU: I encountered a similar situation at my former company. May I tell you what we learned?

ALCHEMIST BOSS: Sure. But can you make it quick? I've got to be in a meeting in five minutes.

YOU: This example isn't exactly the same as what we face here, but it does involve queuing and wait time. I think it's a valuable example.

ALCHEMIST BOSS: Okay. I think have some past experiences that we could use too.

YOU: Great. When I was at Quick Restaurant, Inc., we realized customers were waiting in the drive-up line for more than ten minutes fifteen percent of the time. We investigated a number of different approaches to reducing the wait. Hiring new staff to speed orders was one model. Another was expanding software capabilities to speed up the ordering time. But the one we landed on was contracting with an alliance partner for fill-in staff at peak time. When we examined the cost per transaction, it was the best option.

ALCHEMIST BOSS: So, you think we should hire a contract

>   service for peak call times. But the quality-
>   control issues are still there.
>
> YOU: Not a contract service, but an alliance
>   partner. Someone we could build a long-
>   term relationship with. They would train our
>   operators and we could negotiate an ongoing
>   rate. We'd get better quality and a discounted
>   price. This way we could transfer the call
>   volume to the partner telecom center.
>
> ALCHEMIST BOSS: So, you think we can avoid the quality-
>   control concerns?
>
> YOU: I've already screened a couple of the best
>   partner options. Let me tell you the ideas I
>   have to handle the quality concerns when
>   you get back from your meeting. I'd also like
>   to know what other experiences you've had
>   that would build on these ideas.

The Alchemists' point of reference is their personal experience or an alternative model from another industry. Try to think of lots examples and help them reference analogies. When you bring up examples, it often reminds them of their own, then they feel more comfortable investigating and exploring an idea with you.

Because the Alchemists' style is conversational, you should be prepared to have two or more examples in your back pocket. The discussion may wander, so be prepared to navigate the imagination with them. Be sure you recognize both the similarities and the differences of your analogy. You don't want to get caught serving up a model that will not work.

LANDSCAPING IDEAS FOR FOOLS

A two-step process is helpful when working with Fools.

First, convince the Fool you have identified the heart of the problem. Fools are especially sensitive to the truth of an issue. Explore the potential root causes. What is the nature of the challenge? Dig as deep as you can.

Some folks make the mistake of simply taking an assignment and trying to solve a problem that's been handed to them. They don't question whether the right issue has been identified. Fools expect that you will put your energy to task on the very heart of the problem. Don't mess around with symptoms. Get to the core.

Consider a business artist who has been asked to take on a problem and turn it around. Her boss (whose creative profile is the Fool) asks her for a status report on the issue in a month. A Fool approach might be, "You know what I would rather do is dig around for a week or so and then provide you with an assessment of the root problem. Then we can be sure we're solving the right problem."

The second step is a bit more challenging. Find fresh and clever creative responses through celebrating weakness. Use the principles of inversion, absurdity, or perseverance. Fools want to be surprised and delighted. The bar is high for Fools because they are so good at ideas themselves.

Try to identify the two or three key weaknesses. Then experiment with the wild choices or options before you. Don't consider the limitations yet. You probably know them too well. Practice suspending your disbelief that you can actually do any of the wild ideas. Keep focusing on the three-prong skills of the Fool and see what you discover.

Present Fools with both "close in" and "way out" options. What do I mean by this? Give an option that is a low-medium risk. This is something that is the clever but sensible idea. And then tell them about one of your ideas that is wacky but doable if some limitations were altered. Fools like to know you considered some boundary-breaking ideas.

Let's use our example and see how we might share ideas with a Fool:

> **YOU:** I've been thinking how we might solve the overload calls to the Atlanta telecom center.
>
> **FOOL BOSS:** What have you come up with?
>
> **YOU:** Well, first of all I went down there and roamed the halls a bit and talked to the floor managers and staff.
>
> **FOOL BOSS:** And . . . what's the heart of the issue?
>
> **YOU:** When I was having a lattè with the floor manager, he told me he thought the overload was concentrated in the early evening hours. I thought that was strange because we've been talking about the overload calls coming mostly later in the evening.

FOOL BOSS: Maybe he was on a caffeine high.

YOU: Maybe! I went back to the report history and found the number of calls was higher in the late evening. But I wondered why things were so busy in the early evening.

FOOL BOSS: I've always liked detective work too.

YOU: Then I decided to listen in on a few calls with the call staff. What I noticed is that in the early evening we've got a lot more multiple orders. Customers ordering five, ten, fifteen items and more family-oriented stuff. In the later evening, it's primarily men and women with one or two items. The overflow in the early evening is because our operators are working with people longer. The overflow in the late evening is because of the quantity of calls. This is the real problem. It's not that we have too many calls in the early evening. It's that the calls are going on too long for the staff we have.

FOOL BOSS: Interesting. So . . . ideas?

YOU: Well, I was thinking we have a couple of options. First, what if we hired a contract service to take on the extra volume of calls in the late evening? Then we could switch any extra staff we have to handle the early evening calls.

My other idea is a little out there, but I think it's really possible with some noodling. We've had three episodes of call overload in the last three months. We've spent time and effort in figuring out how to tackle each. Obviously there is cost associated with our troubleshooting and the lost orders. How's this for a wild idea? I propose we shut down all three of our call centers and outsource the entire enterprise to Telecom, Inc. I've done some calculations on how it would work and how much we could save. May I show it to you?

Remember that Fools love the truth. Show them you excavated the truth and then tell them about your ideas. Because for a Fool, imagination is all that counts.

LANDSCAPING IDEAS FOR SAGES

Like Fools, Sages need to know that you've found the core of the issue. It's important to them that you have considered the peripheral information, but once you've assured them you have, dive deep.

Sages are bored with extraneous information. They get irritated when you go on too long about why things are the way they are. Don't drone on about the problem. They expect you'll come to them with an insight—some uncommon thought about common matters. In fact, it's not as important that the insight is correct as it is important that you have one. Show them that you've put your wisdom to work. Bring them a unique interpretation.

Sages can't resist a good story. They are drawn in by it and swept off their feet. But make it simple and be sure that you have an insight at the end. Have a good message in your story or you are sunk.

The manager approaches her boss with a story:

> YOU: I heard about something that's going on in Atlanta. I think you'll find it important.
>
> SAGE BOSS: What's the story?
>
> YOU: Doug Hansen called to tell me that there were call overloads at the telecom center. He said, "Can you get down here right away? We need your help."
>
> I flew down right away. When I got there I noticed Doug was right. About fifty-five percent of the calls were waiting over three minutes for operator service. Usually

this season we are not that busy. What do
you think might be responsible for that
overload?

SAGE BOSS: Usually it's a seasonal weather change that
causes more customers to call.

YOU: Exactly what I thought. But as I started to
investigate, I started to coalesce the complex
information. I found something different. I
checked the sales volumes and we are
running twenty percent higher than
forecasted. Sales per call are up fifteen
percent. The volume of calls is also up. I
decided to answer some phones for myself.
Callers in different parts of the country were
telling me personally how much they loved
this catalog's merchandise! I got unsolicited
praise from two of the four orders I took.

SAGE BOSS: Really? That makes a bad story better.

YOU: Yeah. This is what I think is the essence of
the issue. Our products have touched a chord
with the customer. This season's merchandise
is hot.

SAGE BOSS: What do you recommend we do?

YOU: First, we need to increase call staff just to
handle the load. Next, I think we should do
some in-depth interviewing with key
customers to find out what they like so
much. Let's keep this momentum going!

Sages like a short story with an insightful conclusion. That's it. Short and
sweet. Try not to get sidetracked even by the questions the Sage asks.
Always be prepared enough to bring the discussion back to the key issues.

When you have mastered using all the Five Faces skills, you can learn to
understand how to more effectively communicate with your co-workers
and colleagues and become an idea champion within your organization.

The Death of the "S" Word

Most managers use the word "strategy" to sell ideas. They claim an idea is strategic or on strategy, so the concept will win the head nod of their management. It sounds smart.

But the word "strategy" is overused by almost every corporation. It is in fact so overused, it means next to nothing. Our attempts to look smart are often misguided. Business artists have killed the "S" word and are substituting it for the "I" word—ideas.

Because in a renaissance, in times of great change, breakthroughs often happen from things that don't make sense, or don't look smart. They are just good ideas. When things are moving really fast, you don't have time to write a report about your strategy. The market, the industry, the world can change in the time it takes to gain consensus and approval. Instead of focusing on strategy development, focus on idea development. The way to sell ideas is to develop good ones.

IV

Discovering
Your Genius Within

"Be a gardener.
Dig a ditch,
toil and sweat,
and turn the earth upside down
and seek the deepness
and water the plants in time.
Continue this labor
and make sweet floods to run and noble and
                    abundant fruits
to spring.
Take this food and drink
and carry it to God
as your true worship."

—JULIAN OF NORWICH

YOU probably came to this book to master the Five Faces of Genius because your work, your business, or your firm needs your ideas. Now you have the ability to navigate your business imagination; you have the ability to move your firm ahead, move your career ahead. You have the keys to becoming a business artist.

I hope you have also realized that there is a second equally important reason to use the Five Faces of Genius that has nothing to do with the firm and everything to do with you. The expression of your unique creativity is the fulcrum of personal satisfaction at work. No job is meaningful, no job is a learning experience, no job is worth it, unless you exercise your creative spirit. When you master your imagination you find more joy at work, more confidence in yourself, and more meaning in what you do every day.

Genius Within Is the Path to Joy at Work

While waiting to be selected for jury duty, I met a man who started an on-line business. As we waited over a two-day period, we spent a lot of time together. He explained his new company with what could be described as nothing but joy. He talked about how he was part of a team that created the idea for a new Internet service. He was ebullient about the idea. He had a contagious enthusiasm. In the close quarters of the jury area, I heard him describe his business over and over again to different people. Each time he had the same enthusiasm. It reminded me that creative work produces joy.

The business artist knows that if you don't love what you do at some level—what you're selling at work, what you're learning at work, what your company stands for or even what you stand for in your company—it's almost impossible to innovate. As da Vinci claimed, if our spirit is not part of what we do, we will have no art. We can't move from business manager to business artist without some measure of passion.

Sure, even a passionate manager has low points, slow points, or lack-of-enthusiasm points. But the creative life is built on the rock of passion. Leo Burnett said about advertising, "I'm often asked how I got into this—it got into me." When we are architects of the future, our joy at work buoys us.

You might be thinking, "If only I knew what I wanted to do, then I would be creative" or, "I am jealous of those who know exactly what they want to do with their life. It's easy for them to be passionate." We think lack of fulfillment happens because we haven't found our true calling. We believe if we discovered the right job, we'd be happy.

It is a fallacy that the *content* of our work is the only thing that brings fulfillment. Our joy comes less from *what we do,* but rather *how we do it.* When we make creative and unique contributions in what we do every day, no matter what the chore, we find some purpose in most anything we choose to do. As the mystic Julian of Norwich noted, even digging a ditch or planting a garden can bring fulfillment.

Don't miss creative moments at work because you've convinced your-self they can't happen at *this* job. Be an opportunity hound. Sniff out problems, get some good information, and then guess about solutions. It is dedication to ideas that ultimately makes for joyful work. The stakes are too high not to receive the discipline of genius.

I had a client who seemed so thrilled about his work that I could see his creative genius in our conversation. He had a facility with ideas, with confidence. I asked him how it is that joy is a part of his work.

"There are parts of my job that feel like work. But what really energizes me is this: I'm always trying to find the place where work feels like a hobby. I want what I do every day to be something fun. I sift through my assignments and try to test myself and challenge my creativity. It's always risky, and sometimes I fail, but it's worth it. I spend too much time here for it to be a mental vacuum."

One of my mentors once told me that people are about as happy as they decide to be. If you want to find the joy that comes through creative expression, decide to find it. Put yourself on the path to discovering your genius within.

Here are some approaches you can use to discover the joy of your creative genius at work:

First, examine what binds you. Map out the forces that limit your passion for your work. Is it the field you work in? Your environment? Your coworkers? The hectic life you lead? Use your Observer skills and identify the top five things that bind your creative spirit, then make plans to change each. Often what we feel binds our creativity are, at the heart of it, self-imposed barriers. Our constraints protect us from risking. Imagine you are the All-Powerful One that can eliminate the barriers. See what opportunities for change you discover. Use the space below to do this exercise.

How I might overcome it:

Barrier 1) _____

Barrier 2) _____

Barrier 3) _____

Barrier 4) _____

Barrier 5) _____

Next, use your Seer skills to image what I call the "passion" scenario. What work *would* you feel passionate about? In what environment? With what kind of salary? Create a picture in your mind's eye of some work that feels worthy of your time and talent.

When you visualize a work scenario that builds on your passion, one of two things happens: (1) you see something only slightly different from your current business life or (2) you see something radically different. In the first scenario, you want more responsibility, more reward, more freedom where you are; incremental but meaningful change. In the second scenario, more dramatic life changes are considered—teaching English in China or becoming a biotech researcher. What might your passion scenario look like?

Genius Within Is the Path to Confidence at Work

Leonard da Vinci's biographer called him the "Masterful I." Da Vinci had full mastery of the creative potential inside of him. His curiosity, his passion, his talent all pointed to the expression of something new from nothing. The Five Faces of Genius is meant to make you a "Masterful I." When you exercise your creative spirit, you'll discover wells of confidence you never had.

Over and over I find that low creativity is linked with low personal confidence. You may feel creative in your personal life, but at your core you don't believe you have what it takes to be creative at work. Birthing ideas at home seems less risky. If we sing a lousy harmony to a song, no one needs to know. If we landscape the yard and it fails, it bothers only a few. But our failures at work are highly public, and work is a competitive environment. So the stakes for creativity are raised.

But when we don't risk and fail, our creativity quotient seems to plummet before our eyes. What we expect will save us—being conservative with ideas—in fact sinks us. "I'm not creative, I'm strategic" seems like a safe way to navigate life at work. It's easier to believe we are smart rather than creative, and so the spiral of despair begins.

Sure, some professions have a higher probability of finding creative moments. Answering e-mail for a dot-com company may leave little chance for creative expression. But most work offers moments for individual ingenuity. When you recognize them, cherish them, mold them, and make them more frequent, you grasp stars of satisfaction at work.

It is exactly at the blending of creativity and work that you find confidence. When you experiment with your creative power, you prove to yourself that you can accomplish things. Your role in the world of work matters; you are a creator who brings value. Work transforms from the mundane to something vital. In fact, at work we can find the expression of our true soul.

A client was working in a position that few in the organization valued. Her boss created the job because he thought this function was needed, but no one else did. She spent most of her time justifying her role. She felt her energy draining and her creative spirit wasting away.

When we talked, she said, "I'm ready to leave. If I'm not growing, it's not worth staying." "I agree. If you're not growing, it isn't worth staying. But why is it someone else's responsibility for you to grow? Before you give up, try changing the job from a manager to a business artist. See how you can exercise your creative spirit. What do you have to lose?"

My client took another tack. Instead of fighting to be heard, she started creating and sharing ideas. Sharing with anyone who would listen how the company could grow, opportunities she saw, ideas for customers that needed special attention. She used the Five Faces of Genius to master her business imagination. She became an internal idea resource. People pursued her for teams and special projects. She challenged herself and others found her input more and more valuable. She started contributing. In our next conversation, she said, "Now I'm not just filling a spot. I'm filling my soul."

When we try to become a more inventive person at work, it's scary. We risk the deepest part of ourselves. We've all been part of team where we've shared our best thoughts and no one rallied around us. But the choice is clear. We can risk rejection of our ideas and possibly ourselves, or live a life void of our own creative genius—a life void of joy, a life void of our unique contribution. And making the choice requires courage.

To help you find increased confidence in your genius at work, I'm going to suggest what may seem absurd—a Fool principle—something people tell you not to do. Marry your work. Rollo May says, "A poet marries the language and out of the marriage the poem is formed." In some sense, when we "marry" the business, when we commit to it, we learn to find the poetic solutions. If we have commitment phobia and have trouble being "married" to the *content* of our work, then our creativity falls. We constantly find ourselves questioning where we are, and it distracts us from exercising our imagination. And as you master your imagination, you'll find your creative confidence increasing. Then, surprisingly, you'll be laddering up to more meaningful and fulfilling jobs and careers. *If you can't find moments to be creative in what you do right now, then you'll have difficulty finding them in the next job, too.*

So commit to what you are doing if only for a season. Decide you are going to master your imagination where you are today. Begin in the midst of today. Because it will be the skills you teach yourself today that will catapult you into the future.

What work do you currently do that you can commit your energy to?

_____

_____

_____

Genius Within Is the Path to Meaning at Work

"Sometimes I wonder if life is all about making business presentations." These are the words of a manager reflecting on his current job. He told me he was beginning to believe life was about clocking days in at the office and making one presentation after another. He wondered how life at work could mean more than making a living.

Given the sacred time and energy we commit to work, how do we find purpose in what we do? Is life more than striving? The author David Whyte calls this struggle the "ancient human longing for meaning in work." Can we ever put the words "meaning" and "work" in the same sentence?

The only work worth doing is creative work. The intersection of meaning and labor lies in bringing our creative genius to work. If you want to find purpose in what you do, you have to master your imagination.

Mihaly Csikszentmihalyi says, "Creativity is the central source of meaning in our lives." When we participate in generative activity—that is, when we create something that didn't exist before—we find purpose. When you create something that expresses you—your unique self at work—that's when you're at the intersection of meaning and work called fulfillment.

Most of us have experienced this fulfillment in our personal lives. We've built a deck in our backyard. We nourished a great friendship. We designed a dress from scratch. Created a community charity. Planted a garden. These acts of pure creativity provide us the charge of living. When we give birth to an idea, it's like a drug-induced high.

When we give up on finding our genius at work, we become what I call workhorses. These are managers who are so busy doing, they have little time for ideas. These folks get work "loaded" on their back like a horse. They expect they will get recognized and rewarded for doing more.

Workhorses don't take the business renaissance seriously. When we become workhorses, we don't protect the energy we need to create ideas. We implement the ideas of others. We start taking orders. We put implementation over imagination. We claim work is not an environment that supports creativity. The potential of our creative spirit builds up like the pressure in a grain silo so tightly sealed we cannot release it at work. Our creative soul begins to rot.

Creating ideas is not just for the "luxury" jobs—the executives and senior managers. Creative expression can be a part of any post we hold, from the word processor to the CFO; from small ways to save money, to better ways to help customers; from new ways to track projects to deciding which companies to acquire. The key is to *imagine the opportunities for contribution wherever we are and practice our creativity;* to become more familiar with our own creative genius, to share it with others.

To discover more meaning in your work, use your Sage skills and get to the heart of the issue. Ask yourself, "What do I want?"

The famous psychotherapist Karen Horney said that at the root of personal conflict is confusion about the question "What do I want?" When we become aware of our hearts' desire, we take the first step toward ideas. What do you want from your work? Make a list of the top three priorities you expect from what you do. Is your current career meeting those priorities? What potential do you have to meet them? If you have a significant discrepancy between what you want and what you can have, begin to plan vital steps for your future.

1. What are the top three things you want from work?

1)

2)

3)

2. What steps can you take to make them happen?

1)

2)

3)

Consider the professional who wanted a new career but didn't know what to pursue. She negotiated a three-day-a-week arrangement with her current employer. She used the other two days a week for self-discovery to determine her next career steps.

Sometimes starting all over feels too risky for us. But the truth is, it's more risky to clock precious "life time" in a career that means little. Protecting your purpose for work is one of the most important missions of your life. In the words of the Persian mystical poet 'Attār, "Be more deeply courageous. Change your soul."

Get in a goal-setting habit. Creativity blocks feed on personal conflict. If you are unclear about the meaning of this professional rhythm in your life, you'll lack ideas and feel rudderless.

Every quarter or so, write down your "next step" goals. Many of us have trouble designing a long-term vision for our career. So design a short-term vision. E. L. Doctorow said, "It's like driving a car at night. You never see further than your headlights, but you can make the whole trip that way." Just look at what passions are in front of your headlights. What do you want today?

3. Write down three goals you would like to achieve as a result of the work you've done in this book.

1)

2)

3)

Nobel Prize winner-environmentalist David Brower claimed that as he got older this Goethe quote became his religion. "If you can imagine it, begin it. Boldness has genius, magic, and power in it." At every juncture, at every decision, he strived for the bold move. Meaning in his life has come by way of exercising bold moves.

Make bold your religion—choose the bold decision, the bold projects, the bold careers—and when you do, you'll find meaning in your work and your genius within.

You have the Face of Genius. Within you lies the power to create, to wrest ideas from the heavens, to make something new. Because *you* embody genius—the ability to give birth to ideas.

Now you have the creative strength that Nietzsche called the "overflowing energy that is pregnant with future." One manager says, "The Five Faces of Genius principles give me ways to inspire creativity in myself and others."

Now you can fight for energy at work. You can dampen the voices that call out to "look busy." You can make rituals at work that buoy your spirit of invention. You can organize the priorities of your life to spin around the center of purpose.

Now you know creativity is your birthright. It is your job to create; to grasp those moments of mystery and make of them what you can.

I Create, Therefore I Am

The philosopher René Descartes said the essence of the human spirit is "I think, therefore I am." But Descartes was wrong. It is not our ability to reason that makes us human; it is our ability to create, to call forth ideas from ex nihilo—from nothing.

Richard Feynman said, "We are not that much smarter than each other." I find that comforting from one of the world's most exceptional minds. It's not our ability to reason that makes us who we are; it is our power to create and contribute. Those who make contributions trust their creative fire.

Expect creative fire from yourself. Martha Graham talked about her creative fire as Blood Memory. She believed humans pass creativity from generation to generation through their blood, and that there is an unconscious memory that spurs us to build on the contributions of our foremothers and forefathers. She felt her dances were created by the footsteps of her ancestors.

Blood Memory means that you stand in the tradition of human creativity that has gone before. You stand in the creative tradition of those who painted the Lascoux caves in France. You stand in the creative tradition of those who built Stonehenge. You stand in the creative tradition of the inventors of the printing press. You stand in the creative tradition of those who created the silicon chip. You stand in the creative tradition of your grandmother and grandfather. All of us share in this spirit. Your creative genius is your heritage, your birthright, your gift. Offer it to the world.

I create, therefore I am. Create and find your genius within.

NOTES

Page

10 "When I am, as it were": Astrid Fitzgerald, *An Artist's Book of Inspiration* (Hudson, NY: Lindisfavne Press, 1996), p. 161.

10 "Wouldn't it be fun": Bob Thomas, *Walt Disney: An American Original* (New York, NY: Hyperion, 1994), p. 218.

11 Roy Plunkett's configuration of chlorofluorocarbon: "The Accidental Inventor," *Discover*, October 1996, p. 69.

11 Alfred Stieglitz . . . Enchanted with . . . Vermeer: Richard Whelan, *Alfred Stieglitz, A Biography* (Boston, MA: Little, Brown and Company, 1995), p. 97.

Chapter 1: The Seer

21 "That night in my motel": Daniel Gross, *Greatest Business Stories of All Time* (New York, NY: John Wiley and Sons, 1996), p. 180.

22 "I have things in my head": Sarah Whitaker Peter, *Becoming O'Keeffe: The Early Years* (New York, NY: Abbeville Press, 1991), p. 31.

23 "He wondered how things": Denis Brian, *Einstein: A Life* (New York, NY: John Wiley and Sons, 1996), p. 65.

23 "An idea for a novel": Mihaly Csikszentmihalyi, *Creativity: The Flow and Psychology of Discovery and Invention* (New York, NY: HarperCollins, 1996), p. 115.

24 "Whatever exists": A. Richard Turner, *Inventing Leonardo* (Berkeley, CA: University of California Press, 1992), p. 152.

24 Mozart and Salieri dialogue: Peter Schaffer, *Amadeus*, screenplay. Movie produced by Orion, 1984.

25 "He manipulated the diagrams": James Glick, *Genius: The Life and Science of Richard Feynman* (New York, NY: Vintage Press, 1992), p. 131.

26 "We are going to own": "We Are Going to Own This Generation," *Business Weekly*, February 15, 1999, p. 88.

27 Wayne Huizinga reinventing car buying: "Wayne's New World," *Time*, December 16, 1996, p. 50.

Page

28   "We are in the girl business": Gretchen Morgenson, *Forbes Great Minds of Business* (New York, NY: John Wiley and Sons, 1997), p. 137.

31   3Com's Palm V: "Putting Fluff over Function," *Fortune*, March 15, 1999, p. 163.

31   "I was picturing my arm": "Stopping Diaper Leaks Can Be Nasty Business, P + G Shows Its Rivals," *Wall Street Journal*, April 5, 1999, p. BI.

33   Owens Corning turn around: "Owens Corning Back from the Dead," *Fortune*, May 26, 1997, pp. 118–26.

40   "Creative persons often": Mihaly Csikszentmihalayi, *Creativity: The Flow and Psychology of Discovery and Invention* (New York, NY: HarperCollins, 1996), p. 58.

Chapter 2: The Observer

46   "As his daughter": Bob Thomas, *Walt Disney: An American Original* (New York, NY: Hyperion, 1994), p. 218.

47   Robert Frost's first published poem: Jay Parins, *Robert Frost: A Life* (New York, NY: Henry Holt, 1999), p. 44.

47   "And there were other things": *Frost Collected Poems, Prose and Plays* (New York, NY: The Library of America, 1995), p. 36.

48   "At around age six": Eudora Welty, *One Writer's Beginnings* (Cambridge, MA: Harvad University Press, 1984), p. 10.

49   Leonardo's parties for peasants: A. Richard Turner, *Inventing Leonardo* (Berkeley, CA: University of California Press, 1992), p. 82.

50   "The key to Bob's genius": Bob Spitz, *Dylan: A Biography* (New York, NY: W. W. Norton, 1989), p. 134.

50   "Wherever she went": Jane Howard, *Margaret Mead: A Life* (New York, NY: Fawcett, 1990), p. 14.

50   "Curiosity is the secret": *100 Leo's: Wit and Wisdom from Leo Burnett* (Lincoln, IL: NTC Business Books, 1995), p. 27.

50   "inquisitive question-box": Neil Baldwin, *Edison: Inventing the Century* (New York, NY: Hyperion, 1995), p. 19.

51   "the arbiter of all questions": A. Richard Turner, *Inventing Leonardo* (Berkeley, CA: University of California Press, 1992), p. 62.

51   "the most relentlessly curious man": Kenneth Clark, *Civilization* (New York, NY: Harper and Row, 1969), p. 135.

51   "In my room at Princeton": Richard Feynman, *Surely You're Joking Mr. Feynman!* (New York, NY: W. W. Norton, 1985), p. 94.

Page

51   "the breath of cows": Rosemary Ashton, *George Eliot: A Life* (London: Penguin, 1996), p. 187.

51   "I loaf and invite": Astrid Fitzgerald, *An Artist's Book of Inspiration* (Hudson, NY: Lindisfavne Press, 1996), p. 161.

52   Schultz at Hammarplast: Howard Schultz and Dori Jones Yang, *Pour Your Heart into It* (New York, NY: Hyperion, 1997), p. 25.

52   "I might have become a political cartoonist": Bob Thomas, *Walt Disney: An American Original* (New York, NY: Hyperion, 1994), p. 332.

54   "My mind started churning": Howard Schultz and Dori Jones Yang, *Pour Your Heart into It* (New York, NY: Hyperion, 1997), p. 52.

56   "I've always paid attention to the whispers": "The Three Faces of Steve," *Fortune*, November 9, 1998, p. 104.

56   eBay story: *Wired*, January 1999, p. 69.

56   Levi's and design method: "Dockers Relaxed-Fit Cool," *Fortune*, August 17, 1998, p. 32.

56   Morita watching people: "Akio Morita," *Time*, December 7, 1998, p. 194.

66   3M's 15 percent rule: Rosabeth Moss Kanter, John Dao, Fred Wiersema, *Innovation* (New York, NY: HarperBusiness, 1997), p. 50.

67   "Improvemnets make straight roads": William Blake, *The Norton Anthology of English Literature, 3rd Edition, Vol. 1* (New York, NY: W. W. Norton, 1974), p. 2441.

Chapter 3: The Alchemist

70   Arthur Martinez at Sears: "The Turnabout Is Ending, the Revolution Has Begun," *Fortune*, April 28, 1997, p. 108.

70   Steve Case and AOL and NBC: "Keyword," *Wired*, December 1996, p. 254.

72   Raphael and the Sistine Chapel: Kenneth Clark, *Civilization* (New York, NY: W. W. Norton, 1969), p. 135.

73   "Bob had an ear that was finely tuned": Bob Spitz, *Dylan: A Biography.* (New York, NY: W. W. Norton, 1989), p. 185.

74   "To me, the true artist": J. Krishnamurti, *Total Freedom* (San Francisco, CA: Harper, 1996), p. 43.

75   Leo Burnett and the Malboro Man: Joan Kufrin, *Leo Burnett, Star Reader* (Chicago, IL: Leo Burnett Company, 1995), p. 160.

75   The GAP: "The World According to GAP" *Business Week*, January 27, 1997, p. 73.

Page

75 David Stern and the NBA: "How the National Basketball Association Put the Bounce in Basketball," *Strategy and Business*, Booz-Allen, 3rd Q. 1997, p. 77.

76 "Andy, this is like": Andrew Grove, *Only the Paranoid Survive* (New York, NY: Currency Doubleday, 1996), p. 106.

77 "Joy finds revealing parallels": "Bill Joy," *Fortune*, February 15, 1999, p. 86.

78 Marcy Carsey and Tom Werner story: John Hillkirk and Gary Jacobson, *Grits, Guts and Genius* (Boston, MA: Houghton Mifflin, 1990), p. 44.

79 Peter Lynch and Hanes: Gretchen Morgenson, *Forbes Great Minds of Business* (New York, NY: John Wiley and Sons, 1997), p. 85.

81 "We have found that our peoples' ability": "Unleashing the Power of Learning: An Interview with British Petroleum's John Browne," *Harvard Business Review*, September–October 1997, p. 162.

81 Bill Bowerman and Nike: Donald Katz, *Just Do It: The Nike Spirit in the Corporate World* (Holbrook, MA: Adams Media Corporation, 1994), p. 65.

82 George Eastman story: Daniel J. Boorstin, *The Creators: A History of Heroes of the Imagination* (New York, NY: Vintage Books, 1992), p. 562.

88 "Playing aimlessly with a goal": Clarissa Pinkola Estes, *The Creative Fire: Myths and Stories About the Cycles of Creativity*, (Boulder, CO: Sounds True Recordings, 1991), Tape A21.

Chapter 4: The Fool

90 "Head west and call us tomorrow": "Racing to Round Up Readers," *Smithsonian*, March 1999, p. 83.

93 "Traditional American quilts": Charles M. Johnson, *The Creative Imperative* (Berkeley, CA: Celestial Arts, 1984/6), p. 44.

93 "Out of rot": Joseph Campbell with Bill Moyers, *The Power of Myth* (New York, NY: Doubleday, 1988), p. 102.

94 "I think I may be bold to say": Dava Sobel, *Longitude: The True Story of a Lone Genius Who Solved the Greatest Scientific Problem of His Time* (New York, NY: Penguin, 1995), p. 106.

95 "take one last look": Amir d. Aczel, *Fermat's Last Theorem* (New York, NY: Delta, 1996), p. 132.

97 "Think negative five comp": "GAP Gets It," *Fortune*, August 3, 1998, p. 72.

99 "Is This a Hotel Room or a Broom Closet?": Nancy Keats, *Wall Street Journal*, January 26, 2000, p. B1.

100 Semco story: Ricardo Semler, *Maverick: The Success Story Behind the World's Most Unusual Workplace* (New York, NY: Warner Books, 1993).

Page

101 "I never thought": "Donald Fisher," *Stores*, January 1997, p. 157.

101 Charles "Chuck" House at Hewlett-Packard: David Packard, *The HP Way* (New York, NY: HarperBusiness, 1995), p. 107.

101 Frappuccino story: Howard Schultz and Dori Jones Yang, *Pour Your Heart into It* (New York, NY: Hyperion, 1997), p. 204.

102 "Pick something you really care about": "Apple Gets Way Cooler," *Fortune*, January 24, 2000, p. 71.

103 "NBC sent a clear message": "NBC," *Wired*, December 1998, p. 259.

104 "People usually fail": Astrid Fitzgerald, *An Artist's Book of Inspiration* (Hudson, NY: Lindisfavne Press, 1996), p. 185.

104 Coke and cola war: Barbara and David Mikkelson, *Urban Legends Reference Pages, 1995–2000*, (Internet), p. 183.

110 Lumet and Kurosawa story: Sidney Lumet, *Making Movies* (New York, NY: Alfred A. Knopf, 1995), preface.

112 "unlimited possibilities": Rollo May, *The Courage to Create* (New York, NY: W. W. Norton, 1975), p. 113.

112 Via Negativa: Matthew Fox, *Original Blessing* (Santa Fe, NM: Bear + Co., 1983).

113 "I've very often made mistakes": Richard P. Feynman, *Surely You're Joking, Mr. Feynman!* (New York, NY: W. W. Norton, 1985), p. 83.

114 "One morning as I was lying": Rosemary Ashton, *George Eliot: A Life* (London: Penguin, 1996), p. 166.

Chapter 5: The Sage

115 "The idea for the shop": Anita Roddick, *Body and Soul* (New York, NY: Crown, 1991), p. 69.

116 "Movement never lies": Martha Graham, *Blood Memory* (New York, NY: Washington Square, 1991), p. 8.

116 "When a dancer": ibid, p. 17.

116 "to exclude everything that is unessential": Peter, op. cit., p. 90.

118 "So indescribably beautiful": Amir d. Aczel, *Fermat's Last Theorem* (New York, NY: Delta, 1996), p. 132.

120 Nordstrom's nice people: Robert Spector, Patrick McCarthy, *The Nordstom Way: The Inside Story of America's #1 Customer Service Company* (New York, NY: John Wiley and Sons, 1985), p. 152.

121 "Let's devote all of our resources": "The Rocky Road from Start-Up to Big Time Player, Biogen's Triumph Against the Odds," *Strategy and Business*, Booz-Allen, 1997, Issue 8, p. 62.

Page

123 "We're always looking": "America's Most Admired Companies," *Fortune*, March 3, 1999, p. 71.

125 "Every day I have to make": "Unit of One," *Fast Company*, June/July 1998, p. 84.

126 Crazy Bones: "Toys: Sixty Goofy Looking Little Figures Spark Craze," *Wall Street Journal*, February 4, 1999, p. B1.

128 Land camera: Karen A. Zien and Sheldon A. Buckler, "From Experience Dreams to Market," *Journal of Product Innovation Management*, 14: 1997, p. 275.

129 "I might ask": "How Amazon.com Staffs a Juggernaut," *Wall Street Journal*, April 4, 1999, p. B1.

136 "True genius": Astrid Fitzgerald, *An Aritst's Book of Inspiration* (Hudson, NY: Lindisfavne Press, 1996), p. 4.

Part IV: Discovering Your Genius Within

186 "I'm often asked": *100 Leo's: Wit and Wisdom from Leo Burnett* (Lincoln, IL: NTC Business Books, 1995), p. 108.

188 "Masterful I": A. Richard Turner, *Inventing Leonardo* (Berkeley, CA: Univeristy of California Press, 1992), p. 159.

190 "A poet marries": Rollo May, *The Courage to Create* (New York, NY: W. W. Norton, 1975), p. 85.

194 Blood Memory: Martha Graham, *Blood Memory* (New York, NY: Washington Square, 1991), p. 8.

INDEX

Annette is founder and president of FireMark, an innovation consultancy. FireMark specializes in helping managers unlock their creative genius and apply imagination to business. From her years of research on the nature of creativity, she developed the "Five Faces of Genius" model. This model helps managers bring art to business and develop innovative business solutions. Her inspiring and motivational presentations are well received by audiences all over the country.

Formerly a VP at The Leo Burnett Company, Annette has more than fifteen years of business leadership and marketing experience. She lectures extensively on becoming an artist in the business renaissance. With an MBA from the University of Chicago and a master's of divinity from Princeton Seminary, Annette has combined her experience in business and the arts to develop a popular speaking and workshop practice. To learn more about FireMark services, please visit www.fivefacesofgenius.com